Doug Grad

About the Authors

CLARENCE B. JONES was recruited by Martin Luther King Jr. in 1960 and spent the better part of the next eight years working with him as his principal adviser. He was the first African American allied member of the NYSE who was a principal member of a Wall Street investment banking firm (Carter, Berlind & Weill). The father of five children, Jones lives in Palo Alto, California, where he is a scholar in residence at the Martin Luther King Jr. Research and Education Institute at Stanford.

JOEL ENGEL is the author or coauthor of more than fifteen books. He is a former journalist for such publications as the *New York Times* and the *Los Angeles Times*. He lives in southern California.

WHAT WOULD MARTIN SAY?

WHAT WOULD MARTIN SAY?

CLARENCE B. JONES
AND JOEL ENGEL

HARPER ● PERENNIAL

NEW YORK ● LONDON ● TORONTO ● SYDNEY ● NEW DELHI ● AUCKLAND

HARPER PERENNIAL

HarperCollins books may be purchased for educational, business, or sales
promotional use. For information please write: Special Markets Department,
HarperCollins Publishers, 10 East 53rd Street, New York, NY 10022.

FIRST HARPER PERENNIAL EDITION PUBLISHED 2009.

Designed by Kris Tobiassen

Library of Congress Cataloging-in-Publication Data is available upon request.

ISBN 978-0-06-167267-5

09 10 11 12 13 ID/RRD   10 9 8 7 6 5 4 3 2 1

CONTENTS

In the history of nearly all other races and peoples the doctrine preached at such crises has been that manly self-respect is worth more than lands and houses, and that a people who voluntarily surrender such respect, or cease striving for it, are not worth civilizing.

—W. E. B. Du Bois,
The Souls of Black Folk, 1903

AUTHOR'S NOTE

IN OCTOBER 2007, WHILE IN MEMPHIS, TENNESSEE, I stopped to visit the National Civil Rights Museum. It encompasses the site of the former Lorraine Hotel where Martin Luther King was staying in room 306 on April 4, 1968, as well as the building across the street where his assassin, James Earl Ray, used a telescopic sight to fire the rifle bullet that ended Martin's life.

Leaning out on the balcony through a glass partition outside of room 306, where my friend Martin had been standing that fateful day, I observed an unending stream of visitors from across the nation and around the world. My host and guide, Reverend Samuel "Billy" Kyles, had spent what turned out to be Martin's last hour with him and had, in fact, been standing right there where we were now, on the balcony, when the shot rang out.

Brother Kyles and I talked about Martin's impact on the world and agreed that there was no real way to measure it properly, though he did note how many Nobel Peace Prize laureates had joined countless thousands of other well-wishers to pay tribute at this site: Lech Walesa, Desmond Tutu, Oscar Arias Sánchez, Mikhail Gorbachev, and Nelson Mandela.

What grabbed me most was Rev. Kyles' description of how Mandela had wept as he stood on the spot where Martin died. It brought up all of my own emotion that I'd been either burying or trying to accommodate all these years. The feelings overwhelmed me and I did not fight them.

So it's in that spirit, and with a profound sense of responsibility to both the past and the future, that on the fortieth anniversary of Martin Luther King's death I've tried to interpret what contributions he would add to his singular legacy if he were alive today.

—CLARENCE B. JONES
Palo Alto, California
March 2008

INTRODUCTION

AS ORIGINALLY WRITTEN, THE CONSTITUTION OF the United States was a short, simple document, a dozen pages written in language that the framers considered plain, obvious, and unambiguous. (Even with the seventeen subsequent amendments that have been added to the Bill of Rights since 1789, the entire Constitution still totals fewer than 7,500 words.) It doesn't get much more plain, obvious, and unambiguous than "Congress shall make no law respecting an establishment of religion, or prohibiting the free exercise thereof; or abridging the freedom of speech, or of the press; or the right of the people peaceably to assemble, and to petition the government for a redress of grievances." Nor: "A well regulated militia, being necessary to the security of a free state, the right of the people to keep and bear arms, shall not be infringed."

And yet for more than two hundred years, interpretations of the First and Second Amendments, as well as every other amendment, article, and section of the Constitution, have been tested, questioned, and decided by a Supreme Court that the framers had the foresight to establish as the ultimate arbiter of their own plain words.

Rarely do the Court's nine justices agree unanimously, which of course only ratifies the wisdom of knowing that plain language is in the mind of the beholder. Collectively, Supreme Court justices have written millions of words' worth of opinions on the constitutionality of cases brought before them. Does the people's right to "keep and bear arms" include Uzis, AK-47s, and shoulder-fired missiles? Does "freedom of speech" include the right to shout "Fire!" in a crowded theater—or "nigger" on national television? Does freedom of the press give one the right to willfully publish lies about someone?

These are the kinds of questions the justices answer nine months a year, though their decisions frequently lead to more questions. Some of the most contentious issues dividing the nation's body politic are actually created by the justices themselves, having to interpret a Constitution written by men who couldn't possibly have known that one day there would be birth control pills, surgical abortions, airplanes, television, recording equipment, the Internet, and, for that matter, shoulder-fired missiles.

Just as Madison and Hamilton and the other framers were men of their own time whose worldview was informed by the tyranny against which they'd fought a war, so too do today's justices bring their experiences in modern America to the bench. Some of them believe that the Constitution is a living document that should be interpreted in deference to modern mores and tastes. Others believe in "original intent"—the idea that the Constitution was written in stone and every decision ought to be decided on grounds plowed by the framers. But even the latter use their modern wits to determine what the framers themselves would advise if they were still alive and could hear cases themselves. All of which is to say that those words written more than two hundred years ago are immutable, but our interpretation of them must, by necessity, be updated for every generation.

If they weren't, then the *Plessy v. Ferguson* decision of 1897 would still stand, allowing "separate but equal" facilities by race—and *Korematsu v. United States* will give the feds the right to round up all Mexicans into internment camps if we ever go to war against Mexico.

MARTIN LUTHER KING JR. SPOKE AND WROTE FAR more words than there are in the Constitution—volumes more. But his words, too, were plain, obvious, and unambiguous, written and uttered not to establish a viable republic but to inspire that republic to fulfill its founding ideals. His motivation was moral, not political.

Except for Abraham Lincoln, Martin arguably did more to bring about social and legal justice in America than anyone in the four centuries since colonization of this continent began. He died forty years ago, working for justice until his last moment, and today America honors only one man with a national holiday—Martin Luther King. It's precisely his status as a moral architect—better, a kind of secular saint—that now causes many Americans to wonder what he might have to say on particular issues of the day, much as Christians ask themselves what Jesus would do in a given situation.

Almost every day I hear someone taking Martin's words out of their spoken or written context to prove any point that the speaker intends to make, knowing that Martin's supposed opinion will lend credibility to any argument. Few things irritate me more. Martin Luther King Jr. was no Rorschach test, allowing the beholder to see whatever he chooses to see and believe.

I knew Martin Luther King. I worked closely with Martin Luther King. Martin Luther King was a friend of mine.

I think I understand what he would have to say, and what he would advise, on issues of the day. I think I knew his mind as well as anyone, and in fact as a draft speechwriter and adviser, I did indeed often put words in his mouth. That's why I've volunteered in this book to act as a sort of Supreme Court, to translate Martin for a modern audience concerned with a variety of subjects and looking for the moral leadership that he gave the country during perilous times. These, too, are perilous times.

It's important to remember, as you read, that if it were as simple as quoting Martin on any given topic, then my presence here would be unnecessary. You could simply find a quotation on, say, the Vietnam War and know what to think about Iraq. But, like Court opinions regarding free speech and the right to bear arms, proper analysis demands context, history, and slow deliberation. And that's fitting, because Martin never formed an opinion that wasn't considered.

Some may disagree with the opinions here, just as there are dissenting or minority views on the Supreme Court. But I believe that my interpretation of current events and issues viewed through this prism would be nearly unanimous. I was privy to his innermost thoughts, and my intention is to bring Martin Luther King alive on the page, using what I knew to demonstrate that his moral vision has survived the decades intact and is applicable to the way we live today.

"A nation or civilization that continues to produce soft-minded men," he said, "purchases its own spiritual death on an installment plan."

WHAT WOULD MARTIN SAY?

ONE

WHAT DID MARTIN SAY ABOUT ME?

MARTIN LUTHER KING WAS COMING TO MEET ME. AT MY home. It would be social, but not a social visit. Like Uncle Sam in those recruiting posters, Dr. King wanted to enlist me in his war. But I had already become a conscientious objector.

IT WAS A LONG-AGO TIME AND YET NEVER LONG ENOUGH. It was a time when not the few but the many believed—as surely as they believed that gravity makes things fall—in the racial superiority of the white race. It was a time when more than a few agreed that because man is made in God's image and God isn't black, the Negro is therefore not a man. It was a time when far more than many insisted that the law needed to separate blacks from whites not only today but tomorrow and forever.

It was, in short, a time when the time was ripe for one of those most rare movements in history, a movement whose goals and aims were as righteous as they were unambiguously good.

It also happened to be the time when I was happily living in a scenic white suburb of Los Angeles in a pleasant ranch-style contemporary with my attractive white wife and, less than a year out of law school, working as an entertainment lawyer at a small Beverly Hills firm where I hoped someday to make partner and enjoy all the rights and privileges thereto pertaining—i.e., a lavish salary and everything it could buy. Including the freedom to never again worry about how much I had left in my pocket.

I'd had those plans (born of that worry) since that day as a boy when I learned that my beloved parents—live-in domestics—would have to send their only child away to be raised by others. And now that I had a wife and baby daughter with a second child on the way, I felt a moral obligation to be there for them, both physically and financially. It was, perhaps, a sense of duty best appreciated by those who'd been raised by folks other than their parents. The Catholic nuns in that boarding school run by the Order of the Sacred Heart in Cornwells Heights, Pennsylvania, taught me well, and my success reflected that. But I would always have a hole where my parents hadn't been, and a hole wasn't what I wanted for my children.

That said, unless you were a first-degree bigot, it was impossible not to admire the Reverend Dr. Martin Luther King Jr. And impossible not to notice that he was the right man at the right time. His mission to achieve full civil rights for American Negroes had made him one of the most famous and, even in those days, celebrated men in the United States. He'd actually been on the cover of *Time* after leading the year-long Montgomery bus boycott, begun by Rosa Parks, which eventually led to the Supreme Court's ruling that outlawed segregation on municipal buses. So it was a big deal that he was coming to my house and coming to see me personally and coming to appeal to my conscience and coming to persuade me that I was not, at present, putting my talents to their highest and best use.

But big deal or not, God himself couldn't have persuaded this Negro to give up the future, even for something bigger than himself.

Anyway, that's what I insisted to my wife as she set out a few refreshments before our guest arrived.

Hearing the words, she stopped for a moment and shook her head. Which got *my* attention. In the five years and counting of our marriage, she'd never looked at me so pitiably, as though she'd married the wrong man.

2

The phone had rung several days before—Hubert Delaney, calling from New York. I'd gotten to know Hubert, a prominent Negro lawyer and former judge, during my college days at Columbia, when I was a member of the school's NAACP Youth Council. He'd generously written a letter of recommendation to Boston University Law School on my behalf when I decided to pursue the law, and I have no doubt that whatever he said helped get me in. But not for that reason alone did I owe him.

Even so, when he told me he thought I'd be a good and valuable addition to the legal team he was heading in Alabama to defend Dr. King against preposterous charges of tax evasion—that is, underreporting his income in 1956 and 1958 through the appropriation of donations to the Montgomery bus boycott—I told him no. And not because I didn't want to spend several weeks in Montgomery (though I didn't), acting essentially as a law clerk for several eminent attorneys from the North, writing motions and memoranda, researching case law, and being a legal gofer. No, I didn't want to do that because, well, I didn't want to do that. I wanted to stay where I was and continue doing what I was doing—making money and building my future.

With disappointment in his voice, Hubert thanked me and that was that—or so I thought until the next day, when Dr. King's personal secretary from the Southern Christian Leadership Conference called to say that the man was going to be in Los Angeles over the weekend, delivering the keynote address at the World Affairs Council dinner Saturday night, and would it be possible for him to stop by the house for a brief chat on Friday night after dinner. Just to say hello.

I laughed, marveling that the judge hadn't given up. What was I supposed to say? No?

And so came the knock on the door.

There stood a man of medium stature, wearing a dark suit, white shirt, skinny tie, and fedora.

"How do you do?" he said. "I'm Martin."

Next to him was a man similarly dressed, the Reverend Bernard Lee, King's aide-de-camp.

We shook hands and I invited them in. King first noticed how the house had been built around an existing tree that would've dominated the living room if not for the hundreds of potted plants, courtesy of my wife's green thumb. Then he glanced up at the place where a portion of the roof had been retracted for the night—a nice architectural touch that paid off whenever the stars were alive in the sky, as they were then—and nodded in a way that said I'd done well for myself.

"Pretty nice house you have here, Mr. Jones," he said.

I introduced him to Anne, who'd grown up in New York City, the daughter of a prominent family, so she'd met her share of important people. But in front of Martin Luther King, she seemed awestruck. It's funny, but before he arrived I'd actually wondered whether he'd be shocked to see me married to a white woman—something that was still illegal in most southern states—and whether this, uh, miscegenation would put him off; he was, after all, a southerner himself. But he sure didn't seem put off. He acted gracious and appeared charmed by her.

We sat on the sofa, in front of a table with the snacks she'd put out.

I said, "I'm thankful to Judge Delaney—that he could set this up."

"Hubert had some very nice things to say about you," he said. "Very nice. Very complimentary."

And the small talk went on for some time, about how Dr. King had earned his Ph.D. from Boston University's School of Theology in 1955, the year before I'd entered its law school; about how he'd formed the Southern Christian Leadership Conference about the time I was a first-year law student; about the Montgomery bus boycott and the thrilling Supreme Court ruling; about the success on Broadway of my friend Lorraine Hansberry's *A Raisin in the Sun*; about the coming presidential election and the possible nomination of Senator John F. Kennedy as the Democratic candidate. And about my background as the only child of a maid and a gardener-chauffeur, living with two foster families before ending up at Catholic boarding school, where I took four years of Latin—religious Latin. This clearly interested him.

Then my daughter Christine, who was about a year old, toddled into the room to test her new skill: walking. King played with her delightedly until Anne put her to bed. And at last we got to the point.

"As you know," he said, "I was just indicted by Alabama for perjury—lying on my tax return. They say I was evading taxes. I don't think I have to tell you that I did no such thing, but I'll tell you anyway: I did no such thing."

"You have an excellent legal team—cream of the crop," I said. "I'm sure you'll beat it."

Now he appeared to shift gears, telling me about his trip the previous year to India for meetings with the adherents of Mohandas Gandhi, who had famously been in great part responsible for the British departure from the subcontinent through his policy of religiously devoted nonviolence. Gandhi's tactics and strategies, King said, were directly applicable to America's civil rights movement. He used the word "movement."

What struck me was how much eye contact Dr. King made with Anne while he spoke, as though the way to me was through her. If that were so, I'd have been on the next plane to Montgomery, judging by how entranced she was by everything he said.

"The movement," he said, "is fortunate to have the generous support of many northern white liberals, including lawyers." He paused, possibly to consider telling me about one of his closest advisers, Stanley Levison, a successful white businessman who'd gone back to school to earn a law degree in order to improve his effectiveness as a liberal activist. It was Stanley Levison who'd prepared Dr. King's tax returns, and it was he who'd acted as agent for the book King wrote about the Montgomery boycott. Stanley, it should be pointed out, refused every dime of compensation ever offered him by the SCLC and Martin Luther King; and it's safe to say that if Stanley had ever been convinced that complete civil rights for Negroes could have been accomplished somehow by his own impoverishment and death,

Stanley would've considered it a bargain. (Stanley Levison is someone who deserves a statue for his devotion to Martin and work for the civil rights movement.)

But Dr. King didn't mention him then. He continued: "One of my concerns, however, is our dire need of committed Negro professionals—doctors, accountants, insurance agents. Particularly lawyers. The movement doesn't have nearly enough of them—of people like you. We'd like to see them get more involved with the movement to help our southern brothers and sisters."

I understand, I said, and he explained that he believed there was going to be a concerted effort by the white power structure to intimidate civil rights workers and undermine the movement through the courts. "What they can't do with clubs and dogs and fire hoses and bullets they'll do with lawsuits and criminal cases—try to bleed us dry. This indictment is just the first cut."

Now was the time for me to offer whatever assistance I could in the way of legal research, exploring Alabama case law in local law libraries and sending my results—airmail special delivery!—to Montgomery. "I'm happy to do that," I said, "but I can't leave my family to go to Alabama for weeks or months. I'm sorry."

3

After he left I faced the wrath—actually, the frustration—of Anne Aston Warder Norton Jones, daughter of the late William Warder Norton, better known as W. W. Norton, founder of the eminent publishing house.

Anne's mother was Mary Dows Herter, a cellist, renowned translator of the German poet Rilke, and cultural benefactor whose beneficiaries included Ravi Shankar, Aaron

Copland, and the Manhattan School of Music. Anne's uncle, Christian Herter, had been a congressman, then governor of Massachusetts, and was at that moment President Eisenhower's secretary of state. All of which is to say that Anne grew up quite well, and connected, on Lexington Avenue, in New York City, a fact consistent with her matriculation at the Brearley School for Girls and a bachelor's degree from Sarah Lawrence, though not necessarily her master's degree in social work from BU.

Maybe the most important if not ironic piece of her personal mosaic, at least as it relates to Martin Luther King and me, was that after Anne's father died when she was a teen, Anne's mother (referred to affectionately as "Polly") remarried a major Dutch banker named Daniel H. Crena de Iongh, who'd been an executive and treasurer with the World Bank. His closest business ties were in South Africa, where he and Polly vacationed every winter—which is summer down there—as guests of Hendrik Frensch Verwoerd, the country's prime minister and primary architect of modern apartheid. Over the years, I've often made myself smile by imagining Daniel showing Hendrik his stepdaughter's wedding photos and having to explain that that guy's not the waiter; he's the groom.

Whatever other enlightened, sophisticated instincts she may have had, Anne's mother must have had to swallow hard the first time her well-raised daughter brought this son of black domestic workers to their home in Wilton, Connecticut. To her great credit—remember, this was still the 1950s—she was eminently polite and courteous, asking about my graduation from Columbia University, my military service, and my love for classical music.

"Do you play?" she asked.

I said I'd been playing clarinet since the nuns put one

in my hands at age 8, taking well enough to it that, at 16, I sat first clarinet in the New Jersey State High School Orchestra. My favorite, I said, was chamber music from the baroque and classical periods—as it was Polly's, she said.

Then Polly heard me play, from memory, the adagio movement of Mozart's clarinet concerto in A, one of the most emotionally affecting pieces of music ever written. Tears filled her eyes, and I like to think that Mozart didn't deserve all the credit. In fact, she quickly invited me to play some duets with her and then sit in with her chamber group. We were soon giving recitals in Wilton, in Gramercy Park living rooms, and at the Cosmopolitan Club, where, even in cosmopolitan New York, the Negro help had their own entrance.

Of course, looking back—with irony and maybe a little cynicism, though not bitterness—the story reflects its own kind of insidious racism: the black man essentially having to perform card tricks before being "good enough" for the white woman's white daughter. It was the kind of sentiment dramatized a full ten years later in what was then a landmark movie, *Guess Who's Coming to Dinner*: Sidney Poitier couldn't have been anything less than a distinguished physician before even trying to convince Spencer Tracy and Katherine Hepburn that he was worthy of their daughter.

But regardless of the genteel racism, I know for certain that my late mother-in-law was transformed utterly by the birth of her first grandchild, my first daughter. We were side by side in the waiting room in Boston when the doctor walked in and said, "Mr. Jones, you're the proud father of a beautiful baby girl." Mrs. Crena de Iongh spontaneously, and uncharacteristically, hugged me. It may have been one of the most authentically spontaneous moments of her life. (During all the years of my marriage to Anne, she treated me with affection and respect and loved Christine and her other grandchildren, Alexia Norton, Clarence Jr., and his brother Dana, as much as she loved anyone.)

That potential was what Anne knew about her mother before her mother knew it about herself, and it's what she believed of all people, that if you showed them the path of righteousness, they would eventually choose to walk down it themselves—exactly what Martin Luther King believed and practiced.

Which was why Anne was so disappointed in me after he left.

"What are you doing that's so goddamned important you can't go off for a few weeks to help him?" she said. "The man came all the way here to meet you—to ask you personally."

"Come on," I said, "just because some Negro preacher got his hand caught in the cookie jar, it's not my problem." Needless to say, this was not my finest moment.

Anne was furious. "You mean you think he really did it? Shame on you."

It was a long night between my wife and me—but not a long dark night of the soul. I felt comfortable with my position. Truly, God himself couldn't have dissuaded me.

And he didn't.

4

Saturday morning I got another call from Dr. King's secretary in Atlanta, this time inviting Anne and me to attend Sunday services at a Baptist church in Baldwin Hills where he was to be the guest preacher before returning home. I laughed, admiring his doggedness, and said we'd be pleased to be there. Anne, though, didn't feel well enough. "You may not be going to Montgomery," she told me, "but you are definitely going down there to hear Dr. King speak."

So I went alone.

About half an hour away on the freeway, Baldwin Hills was like the black Beverly Hills of Los Angeles, an area somewhat north of the airport where well-to-do professionals and entertainers like Nat King Cole lived. The church held probably 2,000 worshippers, and its parking lot was thrillingly decorated, of course, by Cadillacs, as well as Lincolns, and even, no kidding, a few Rolls-Royces. Obviously, more than one or two Negroes were doing just fine in Los Angeles in the late winter of 1960.

Someone escorted me to my seat in the twentieth row, just behind the church trustees, deacons, and other VIP guests. Every other seat was filled. Those who hadn't been there since the previous Easter had now come to hear the great man speak, and when the church's presiding pastor, Rev. H. B. Charles, turned over the proceedings to Dr. King, no one missed a syllable for the next hour.

"Brothers and sisters," he began, "the text of my sermon today concerns the role and responsibility of the Negro professional to the masses of our brothers and sisters who are struggling for civil rights in the South."

With a natural storyteller's ease, he related how the Montgomery bus boycott Supreme Court decision had galvanized tens of thousands of ordinary southern Negroes to begin to think of themselves as human beings—and how, if you visited the South now, you could just sense that a new day was coming.

I leaned forward in my seat, eager to hear whatever came out of this man's mouth. With just these few words, witnessed in person instead of heard over the radio or quoted in the newspaper, I realized I'd never heard anyone so thoroughly capable of transfixing the listener. It was magic. What Frank Sinatra was renowned for doing with his singing voice, the Reverend Dr. Martin Luther King Jr. did with his speaking voice. The phrasing was immaculate, his inflection giving you half the story by itself. The hair on the back of my neck stood up, and I was glad that Anne hadn't come; she'd have been elbowing me in the ribs as she figured out long before I did what the point of his sermon was.

To me, King had chosen the right venue for such a sermon. It occurred to me that there might not have been another black Baptist church anywhere else in the country where his message could've reached so many targeted ears. *Brilliant,* I thought. *This guy King is pretty smart. I get it. At least I see what he wants to do. I get what the big deal is.*

Actually, I hadn't yet. I just didn't know I hadn't gotten it.

He spoke of those Negroes who'd been fortunate to become doctors and lawyers and accountants and performing artists—and what they morally owed those black adults, especially in the Jim Crow South, who never had the chance to do what they did; and those black children who could never by themselves rise above poverty and indignity. It was powerful stuff made poignant when he noted the "literally hundreds of offers" from white northern professionals, particularly lawyers. What a shame it was, he said, that the kindness, generosity, and good will of those whites, while dearly appreciated, was not dwarfed by the kindness, generosity, and good will of those Negroes most in a position to offer them *to their own people.*

Then came a brief pause.

"For example," he continued, "there is a young man with us in this church today who my respected friends and colleagues in New York tell me is a highly gifted attorney. They tell me that this young man's brain has been touched by God. He is so excellent, he can walk into any law library in this country and, in minutes, find cases and citations that an ordinary lawyer wouldn't find even after a full day of looking. They tell me that then, when this young man writes it down in support of a legal argument, his words are so compelling and persuasive that they all but jump off the page."

For a moment, but only for a moment, I wondered whether this young lawyer he was talking about was me. But it couldn't have been. The lawyer Martin described obviously had skills far beyond mine. I decided I had to meet this man before leaving church.

Then came the diamond bullet of recognition, right between my eyes: "This gentleman," Dr. King continued, "lives in a suburb of Los Angeles in a fine, fine home—a home with a tree in the middle of the living room and a ceiling that opens up to the sky."

Uh-oh. Oh, no, dear Lord.

"I recently had a chance to meet this man," he said as I sank down in my seat, trying to hide. "He has a convertible automobile parked in his driveway and a lovely family."

Martin Luther King never looked directly at me, though he ended up making eye contact with everyone else there, or so it seemed as they reacted to his words the way only black folk know how do in church, with oohs and aahs and amens and hallelujahs and other assorted verbal punctuations.

"But," he continued after another dramatic pause, "I'm afraid that this gifted young man has forgotten from whence he came."

Now you could hear hundreds of people tsk-tsk-ing, or women muttering mm-mm-mm in a way that means "for shame."

I tried to shrink further in my seat, feeling like Dr. King

was the only one there *not* looking at me. Of course, it wasn't true; no one else could've known whom he was referring to. But the shame of recognition felt like a theatrical spotlight. And a knife in my belly—one that I held myself.

He said, "And he told me that his parents were domestic servants, his mother a maid and cook, his father a chauffeur and gardener. So here was this Negro woman, working in a white woman's house, who had to send her boy away to live with others, telling him, 'Life ain't easy, son. But you can't give up. I'm doing this for you.'"

Hearing my mother quoted in the exact words I'd remembered, my mind began running a movie of Mom's life, her hard life, her heartbreaking life, her life that ended at 52 of cancer, with pitifully few days of pleasure—days that didn't even include her ultimate dream of seeing her only child's college graduation.

Any parent knows that having to send a child away is an incessant and nearly unendurable pain, one that I was too immature to understand; at the time I believed the pain of separation to be my mine only. Not till later—and too late to say thank you—did I realize that I'd been the lucky one.

Now a second movie began, this one starring every other Negro mother, generations of them, who did as well as possible under the circumstances, all sorts of circumstances, few of them good. Their words of advice weren't always heeded, but they insisted that their children get an education—the education they hadn't had access to. Those children who didn't heed them and those who did soon learned the hard way why education was so important: because a Negro had to be twice as good to be considered half as good as a white. You couldn't argue with that hard-and-fast rule the way you couldn't argue with the laws of physics. As Mom said, "Life ain't easy, son. But you can't give up."

This all would've been painful and persuasive enough if Dr. King had ended just there. But he didn't. In closing he recited the Langston Hughes poem titled "Mother to Son." I'd long ago memorized the words and lip-synched them as he spoke.

> Well, son, I'll tell you:
> Life for me ain't been no crystal stair.
> It's had tacks in it,
> And splinters,
> And boards torn up,
> And places with no carpet on the floor—
> Bare.
> But all the time
> I'se been a-climbin' on,
> And reachin' landin's,
> And turnin' corners,
> And sometimes goin' in the dark
> Where there ain't been no light.
> So, boy, don't you turn back.
> Don't you set down on the steps.
> 'Cause you finds it's kinder hard.
> Don't you fall now—
> For I'se still goin', honey,
> I'se still climbin',
> And life for me ain't been no crystal stair.

Tears rolled off my cheeks, which might've given me away as the culprit if the feeling hadn't come on so many others, too. Only a few were dry-eyed.

Cries of hallelujah and amen mercifully ended the service. People filed out of the pews, and the line up the aisle moved slowly, with dozens stopping at the back to thank Martin Luther King and get his autograph. No question, he was the black Elvis.

At last came my turn. He saw me coming and smiled like a man holding a winning Irish Sweepstakes ticket or like a Cheshire cat who'd just cornered a juicy mouse. I smiled too, but not quite so ingenuously. My smile was, well, sheepish.

"I hope," he said, "that you didn't mind me using you to make a point in my sermon. There were a lot of people here in this church I needed to reach today, and I always use whatever I think is going to be most effective. No offense, Mr. Jones."

"Dr. King," I said, "the only thing I need to know is when you and Judge Delaney want me to leave."

5

These were eventful days, with the Cold War, the growing rock and roll culture, and the civil rights movement seeming to feed off each other in a way that defined the word "symbiosis." Almost everything significant that happened in the United States at that time somehow fell, even tangentially, into one of those three categories. For instance, in the month of May 1960, which culminated with Dr. King's trial and quick acquittal (by an all-white jury, it should be noted), the Soviets shot down an American spy plane piloted by Francis Gary Powers—a humiliating embarrassment for the United States, given that President Eisenhower had denied the plane's existence even as the Russians held Powers in captivity. Meanwhile, Alan Freed, the Cleveland disc jockey who'd coined the term "rock 'n' roll" (appropriating the lyrics of an early "race" song), was arrested for doing what most other disc jockeys were probably doing: taking bribes from record companies in exchange for playing certain records. Everything, it seemed, left a wake of some kind—ripples in a pond that intersected and created new ripples.

I'd been back home in California for less than a week—a hero to my wife—when the phone rang. This time it was Stanley Levison, whom I'd gotten to know reasonably well in Alabama.

He said, "Martin was really taken with you."

"He was?"

"He wants you to know that next weekend the SCLC is having an organizational planning meeting in New York. It's going to be just some key members of the organization."

"And?"

"And Martin would like to invite you."

I chuckled. "Stanley," I said, "I've barely been back a week. I have a job, and I'm lucky to still have it after I took off all that time in Alabama."

"We'd just like you to help us, Clarence. Martin would like you to help us."

"I'm sorry, Stanley," I said. "I was glad to do what I could. But I don't have time for anything else. Not right now. Maybe later."

"I understand," Stanley said. "I'll tell Martin."

The next day the phone rang. A woman's voice said, "Please hold for Dr. Martin Luther King."

"Clarence," Dr. King said. "How are you? You know we're having this meeting, and I'd really appreciate your helping us out. We already have an airline ticket for you to fly to New York. You'll come in early Friday evening, the meeting's all day Saturday and Saturday evening, and you'll be home by Sunday night. Or Monday."

"Dr. King," I said, "I don't know."

"Clarence," he said with an audible wink and a nod, "don't make me go and give another sermon about you."

Checkmate.

The meeting held in a large Harlem loft operated by labor leader and local NAACP president Joe Overton was, I should point out, attended by many whites.

That fact, according to today's climate, would be perceived by a lot of people as inherently wrong. In the early twenty-first century, political correctness holds that white people ought not be making strategic and tactical decisions regarding the future of black people. Which just goes to prove how silly political correctness can become, because everything that discourages conversation retards progress. That, anyway, was Martin Luther King's perception. He rightly understood that blacks and whites share the same destiny and ought to be talking together about how to get both to the promised land of equal opportunity.

At the time I wasn't at all offended by seeing how many of Martin's closest advisers were white. My own perception was that it meant the Movement—capital M, by now—was entirely winnable. After all, since black Americans were about 12 percent of the population, the math alone suggested that defeating prejudice and bigotry required the eventual acquiescence and goodwill of the prejudiced and bigoted. If they didn't ever capitulate—as Martin believed they would, one by one by one—the numbers would always be unbeatable. So it was important to see and know—and for *all* blacks to see and know—that not *all* whites were the enemy.

Of course, no one had to spell that out for me. I'd already accepted from my own coming of age in an overwhelmingly white school administered entirely by white nuns that the average Caucasian was not inherently the Great White Bigot who woke each morning wondering how he could mash his boot on the black man's neck. Indeed, Stanley Levison, in his passion for and devotion to a just society for all Americans, was far from alone. Famous or not, working directly in the Movement or not, there were countless whites of goodwill just waiting to be invited and activated—for example, the hundreds and thousands of otherwise anonymous Freedom Riders and volunteers who would soon begin showing up down South to link arms with their black brothers and sisters, lending both moral and physical support.

Martin Luther King recognized that demonizing whites wasn't just wrong; it was counterproductive. Unlike some people—too many, frankly—he preferred to succeed in his noble goal as opposed to operating in a way that, subconsciously or not, validated why winning was impossible. He saw, as Lincoln had, that he'd do best to appeal to the better angels of the other side's nature—essentially what Gandhi had done in India with the English. By not resisting their evil, Gandhi forced the English eventually to look into a mirror and see their actions for what they were. True, if the oppressors hadn't had consciences—that is, better angels—if they'd all been little Hitlers, no amount of mirrors reflecting their shameful acts would've carried the day. But just as Gandhi had believed in the inevitable goodness of the English, Martin was betting on the basic decency of Americans.

As I recall, I uttered relatively few words at that meeting over its two and a half days, and yet whatever I said must've been impressive enough for me to walk out of there with an assignment for which I hadn't volunteered: co-coordinator, along with Jack O'Dell, of a mass demonstration at the upcoming Democratic National Convention where John F. Kennedy would, it appeared, be chosen as the party's candidate. Why me as co-coordinator? I assume because the convention was to be held in Los Angeles. Why Jack? I frankly don't know, aside from his brains and talent and dedication. Jack was one of those young black southerners who'd returned from World War II wondering why he'd risked so much overseas for a country that held him in such low esteem back home.

My job, on behalf of Martin, was to bring together the chapters of the various civil rights organizations in Los Angeles. It turned out to be an invaluable education on the differences between the NAACP, the SCLC, CORE, and other sometimes disparate groups.

As it happened, I also had to travel frequently for meetings in New York, where I got to know A. Philip Randolph, the great civil rights advocate and labor organizer, then in his seventies, who despite several notable accomplishments may always be best known for organizing black sleeping-car porters—who did the hardest and most thankless job on a train—into a viable and productive union in the 1920s.

"Young Brother Jones, my young friend," he used to say, adapting Lord Palmerston's famous axiom, "don't you know, we Negroes have no permanent friends and no permanent enemies? We Negroes only have permanent interests. Your friend today can be your enemy tomorrow, and vice versa. So don't be worried about aligning with any particular political party."

The goal of our protest outside the new Los Angeles Memorial Sports Arena, where the Democrats were holding their convention, was for jobs and equal employment opportunities—and simply to be noticed and acknowledged. And the way we planned to do that was by marching our long line of protesters around and around the circular building.

I'm not sure whether the symbolism of Jericho was intentional, but the figurative wall did tumble down when the chairman of the Democratic National Committee, Paul

Butler, came out to meet with us and handed out several observer tickets for the convention floor.

Don't judge this incident by modern standards; by modern standards it seems like a pat on the head. Judge it the way Martin Luther King did at the time: as a substantive victory for the Movement. We had gotten our foot literally in the door, and Martin was pleased.

For me, the demonstration turned out to be the last real time I could call Los Angeles home.

6

My presence was now urgently required in New York and elsewhere to coordinate the libel lawsuit filed against the executive board of the SCLC—Joseph Lowery, Ralph Abernathy, Fred Shuttlesworth, and Solomon Seay. In April they'd taken out a full-page ad in the *New York Times* hoping to raise funds for Martin's tax evasion defense as well as the legal defense of four black students who, in February, had refused to observe the "whites only" sign at a North Carolina lunch counter. The ad, titled "Heed Their Rising Voices" and written mostly by Stanley Levison on behalf of the defendants who signed it, was a lengthy recounting of several racial injustices then in the news, including the Montgomery boycott. Most of the particulars had been taken directly from reports in the *Times* by their southern correspondent Claude Sitton, which was ironic given that the paper was also named in the suit filed by Alabama governor John Patterson and Montgomery police chief L. B. Sullivan.

By any measure, this was a petty-ass case, the kind that would either not be filed today or immediately tossed out as frivolous by a judge angered at the waste of his time. In alleging libel the suit claimed that the authors and newspaper willingly and knowingly printed inaccuracies that were, per se, defamatory. Here were the so-called inaccuracies: the ad noted that Negro students on the steps of the state capitol had sung "My Country, 'Tis of Thee," when in truth they'd sung "The Star-Spangled Banner." Then the ad got the *day wrong* on which students had led a demonstration at the Capitol *not* for being expelled by the state board of education but for protesting poor service in the Montgomery courthouse. And instead of the "entire student body" protesting the expulsion of the students, only the vast majority did so. Etc.

Petty or not, the suit confirmed Martin's belief that the greatest weapon against civil rights was not a fire hose but a lawyer on the wrong side of history. He came to see clearly that the ultimate goals were to silence, bankrupt, and decapitate the political leadership of the Movement and intimidate the northern press. Which meant that this suit would not go away by itself. It would have to be won—and decisively—to act as a deterrent against future suits. So a lot was riding on this.

As head of the SCLC, Martin suggested that Stanley and I first meet with the counsel for the *New York Times*—Lord, Day & Lord, a WASPy, white-shoe, staid, conservative law firm if ever there was one—"to see what their thinking is." We did, and in our opinion, their approach to the defense was not good thinking, considering that the paper was flimsily being accused of not fact-checking a paid advertisement based on its own reporting that had gone unchallenged. In not so many words, the lawyers signaled that the most important newspaper in the country would be willing to issue a retraction in mitigation of damages—and, if necessary, settle out of court on a sum that would dismiss only the paper from the suit, thus strengthening the arguments against the others. We had to hold them off, and not just because the so-called Newspaper of Record apparently didn't grasp the enormous First Amendment consequences of capitulation. (Just one example: If it had capitulated, a dozen years later the precedent might have prevented publication of the Pentagon Papers, or at the very least it would've given the editors third, fourth, and fifth thoughts, and their lawyers at the time would've pointed to *Sullivan*.)

Traveling to the South, I met individually with the defendants—Lowery, Abernathy, Shuttlesworth, and Seay—and apprised them of how much more serious this issue was than it then seemed to them, noting that there were soon likely to be judgments against their personal assets. That this assignment should have fallen to me is an indication of how vital I had somehow made myself.

And there was the rub. By early 1961 I had to admit that the Movement was like quicksand from which I'd never escape. Nor did I want to. But keeping the status quo meant spending far too much time on planes and almost never seeing my wife and children. A better alternative, I decided, was relocation to New York. Martin, for one, was pleased. I told him before I told my wife. As it turned out, she needed neither persuasion nor incentive. True, a woman without a modest—emphasis on "modest"—trust fund might've been less willing to give up the promise of security for the glory of the greater good. But knowing Anne's character I have to believe that even if she'd been born to paupers, her enthusiasm for packing up and facing the unknown in the service of a just cause would've been the same.

The favorable price we got for our house in Altadena allowed us to move into an apartment building in Riverdale—the Beverly Hills of the Bronx—where I became friendly with a neighbor named Theodore Kheel, who was a well-known labor lawyer. I mentioned to him one day that we'd moved to New York in part so that I could coordinate the defense of this case. "What I really need to do," I said, "is find some way to build up mass support for our side."

"Hmmm," he said. "Do you think it might help if I arranged a lunch convention for some big New York attorneys? Maybe you could enlist them."

I said that sounded promising.

"Do you think we could get Martin Luther King to speak?"

I said I was sure it could be arranged.

And so it was. Thanks to Ted as well as the work and contacts of Harry Wachtel (a corporate lawyer I'd introduced to Martin, later to become a member of his inner circle), at least fifty top attorneys heard Martin's impassioned argument that "the defense of this case is necessary to the defense of democracy in America." And then, with few if any exceptions, they volunteered to work pro bono.

One of those volunteers was William P. Rogers, who'd just spent four years as Eisenhower's attorney general (and would, at the end of the decade, begin nearly five years as Nixon's secretary of state). It was his prestigious firm, Rogers and Wells, that took on the case, an affiliation that no doubt caused the *New York Times* and its lawyers to develop a stronger spine. Appeal followed appeal, and the case finally reached the Supreme Court in 1964. When the good guys prevailed, it established the modern "actual malice" standard that today gives the press freedom to report on public figures without fear of defamation suits unless the story was published "with reckless disregard" for the truth.

If only that had been the last battle.

7

Day by day, little by little, I became someone on whom Martin Luther King depended for advice. Like any good general or political leader, he solicited the opinions of those in his inner circle before making decisions, and somehow I found myself in the center of that circle, more trusted all the time.

I was not, I should point out, always right. For instance, my estimation of John F. Kennedy and his brother Robert's Department of Justice were overly optimistic regarding enforcement of civil rights, as was proved not for the first time when I predicted that the Kennedy administration would jump to the aid of those trying to desegregate the city of Albany, Georgia. It did no such thing, at least not with alacrity.

Even so, Martin made clear that I was someone whose opinions mattered—to the point where I even began writing many of the speeches, along with Stanley Levison, that came out of his mouth; and because that's where they came from, they changed history. More than forty years later, I say that with as much amazement as pride, the same as any reader would who has come to admire this man and what he stood for.

For his role in one of the Albany demonstrations, Martin would be arrested, convicted, and sentenced to either forty-five days in jail or $178 in fines. The city naturally hoped that he would pay the fine and get out of town without making a fuss, but of course Martin properly, for the sake of the Movement, chose jail.

Between the time of his arrest and jailing, we traveled several times to Albany, hoping to accomplish there what he'd accomplished in Montgomery. Usually we took advantage of Dr. W. G. Anderson's hospitality, sacking out in an attic bedroom that had twin beds—pleasant though hardly posh surroundings for which we were grateful. After one particularly grueling day of strategizing and planning, I stood in my skivvies, hanging up my suit pants, while Martin stretched out on his bed in an undershirt. Feeling bone-tired and not a little homesick, we got on the subject of family and wondered what price our wives and children would pay for our devotion to this cause. Both of us agreed that we'd married the right women—understanding and supportive—but that children can't be expected to appreciate why Daddy not being there is a good thing. The subtext was that we were all paying a price.

"There's something I want to tell you," he said, sitting up. "Anyone can stand with you in the warmth of a summer sun. But only winter soldiers stand with you in the snow at midnight in the Alpine chill of winter." Pause. "You, you and Stanley, you're like wintertime soldiers."

I choked up at these words from this man, and reflexively started to say I didn't fit the description and anyway was no saint. But Martin put up his hand to preempt me.

Martin Luther King knew there were no saints, only men. He knew that I had other options in life but that I chose to be there. And he knew I would recognize his conscious echo of Thomas Paine's famous call to arms: "These are the times that try men's souls. The summer soldier and the sunshine patriot will, in this crisis, shrink from the service of their country; but he that stands it now deserves the love and thanks of man and woman. Tyranny, like hell, is not easily conquered. Yet we have this consolation with us, that the harder the conflict, the more glorious the triumph."

I wish I could say that the Movement, like the Revolutionary War, ended with the glorious triumph that Paine and Martin hoped for. But since those first great battle victories it's been more like an ongoing struggle with no end in sight, only the promise of endless debate.

No doubt Martin would applaud much of the progress we've made in the four decades since his death. But there's also much that would dismay him. Either way, he'd have a great deal to say about a great many things, and much of it might surprise people at every point on the political spectrum who've co-opted his words to suit their agendas.

As one of his winter soldiers, I believe I owe it to him—and to the vision of the just world for which he lived and died—to imagine what kind of leadership and advice Martin would offer us today. April 1968 seems so long ago. I have no doubt that the man, had he lived, would've changed with the times. But the times would've been changed more by the man.

TWO

WHAT WOULD MARTIN SAY ABOUT TODAY'S BLACK LEADERSHIP?

IT WAS 1960. JOHN KENNEDY WAS RUNNING FOR PRESI-dent and much of Hollywood's elite was happily campaigning for the young senator. I believe this was the first time that famous actors had ever campaigned so openly and enthusiastically, which may have been a reaction to Kennedy's opponent. Richard Nixon, the vice president, had been chosen for the ticket by Eisenhower in 1952—a time when the fear of communist infiltration was like a fever in the country—because of his viciously anticommunist credentials. As a two-term congressman in the late 1940s, he'd been a member of the infamous House Un-American Activities Committee that damaged so many Hollywood careers; and then, running for Senate against the wife of noted actor Melvyn Douglas, he all but accused Helen Gahagan Douglas of taking orders directly from Stalin. Nicknaming her the "Pink Lady," he said she was "pink right down to her underwear"—and he wasn't joking.

That kind of tactic could work then. In any event, Hollywood hated Nixon (and always would), and now that the studio system was dying and the bosses could no longer keep their most famous faces from possibly alienating one half of the country by rooting for the other half—politically, that is—the actors weren't afraid to show their support for JFK. I think if Attila the Hun had been Nixon's opponent, they'd have supported him, especially if he was as handsome and rich as the young senator.

Among JFK's ardent admirers was Frank Sinatra, possibly America's most famous and successful entertainer, and his buddies known affectionately as the "Rat Pack"—Dean Martin, Sammy Davis Jr., Joey Bishop, and Peter Lawford, who was in fact JFK's brother-in-law (married to Pat Kennedy). Sinatra performed at several JFK benefits and got to know another JFK supporter and performer, Harry Belafonte, the singer who had stood with the Movement and Martin Luther King since Montgomery. Knowing Sinatra's stand on civil rights—in the 1940s he'd refused to stay in any hotel where blacks like his buddy Sammy couldn't stay too—Harry had no trouble convincing him to sing at a benefit for Martin Luther King and the SCLC at Carnegie Hall. It was a huge success and the Kennedy campaign, apparently feeling some proprietary ownership of Sinatra, believed that reciprocation was called for, as in, "Hey, our guy came through for you, so now your guy should come through for us"—and the guy who was supposed to come through for them was Martin. The Kennedys wanted him to speak at a star-studded gala fundraiser to be held in Beverly Hills, and dispatched Sammy Davis Jr. to bring him back.

Martin said no, and we drafted a letter, with Harry's assent, to explain why.

Here's the reason: We had long ago decided Martin Luther King ought to, as actors used to, remain politically impartial and nonpartisan in order not to alienate the other side. It seemed stupid and shortsighted to align too closely with a party, the Democrats, that might not be in power and therefore able to effect the kind of leadership on civil rights we were looking for from the president of the United States. If Nixon had won, we'd have expected the Republicans to pursue aggressive civil rights bills, just as we did with JFK in the White House. (In fact, Eisenhower had sent to Congress and, against the objections of Democrats, signed into law the Civil Rights Act of 1957, the first civil rights legislation since Reconstruction; it allowed federal prosecutors to go after anyone interfering with another's right to vote.) If Martin had demonstrated favoritism for one campaign over another, it would have been difficult for Nixon, had he been elected, not to perceive Martin as a Kennedy man and therefore shun him.

Sammy came back and pleaded so often, trying to bring home the prized catch for his side, that at last Martin joked I should show up in his place. "You're a California guy," he said. "You're comfortable around all those celebrities."

I said I'd probably end up saying something irreverent and getting us all in trouble.

"Better you than me," he said, meaning that his position as America's foremost Negro leader forced him to be exquisitely careful about being manipulated by politicians.

Today, sadly, many of America's so-called black leaders appear to excel at being manipulated by politicians, mostly Democrats—for whom blacks vote reflexively, almost religiously. In essence, black America has become a wholly owned subsidiary of the Democratic Party, with African Americans convinced that to vote for another party is akin to endorsing the Klan. As the most reliable Democratic Party bloc, blacks mark their ballots for the Democratic candidate, on average, more than 90 percent of the time. So, like the lovesick girl who makes herself far too available to the object of her affection, blacks are taken for granted and ignored by Democrats until it comes time to vote. Indeed, the analogy holds there too, given that the young man with the lovesick girl pays attention to her only when he's in the mood for some good thing. To Democrats, that good thing is an X on the ballot. (And for inexplicable reasons, not nearly enough blacks feel insulted by the patronizing way white candidates generally address black audiences, in that awful "street" accent of theirs, as if they thought pretending to be down in the 'hood made them more authentic. It doesn't. It makes them pandering phonies, as when Hillary Clinton trots out that drawl and says, "And you know what I'm talkin' 'bout." Does anyone expect Americans to speak in a German accent when they address the Bundestag or, for that matter, like Speedy Gonzales when they speak before Mexican Americans? Why is it only African Americans get this special treatment? Seems to me, and I know it would seem to Martin, that it reflects a kind of racism—the idea that blacks have to be spoken to in what's essentially baby talk, like mommies to their infants. Do you know what I'm talkin' 'bout?)

This situation creates political irony and sadness galore, because this manipulation is done not just with the acquiescence of black leaders; it's done, it appears, with their consent and approval. What compelling evidence is there to disprove the otherwise obvious inference that theirs is the most cynical kind of manipulation, one meant to enhance their checkbooks and prestige as power brokers capable of delivering their people—less for their people's interest than their own? If the actions of these leaders were really in the people's interest, they would read a Negotiation 101 textbook and pursue all options with Republicans, too, rather than demonizing the GOP as an eternal racist enemy. Then blacks would be in the driver's seat on several major issues, including illegal immigration, which affects them disproportionately through a loss of jobs that had been traditionally black. Since no national Democratic candidate has a chance of getting elected without the black vote, blacks would be in a position to dictate the terms of debate, and maybe even end all debate by insisting that the border be closed and everyone sent home. Overnight, jobs would be freed and wages rise, especially for those at the lower end.

Intentionally or not, current black leaders seem to pursue policies that pimp the best interests of black people. Convincing blacks that they've been born with one foot in the grave, or are hopelessly disadvantaged in politics and economics, only works to make names and fortunes for power brokers perceived as being able to reliably deliver that black vote to councilmen, aldermen, mayors, assemblymen, congressmen, senators, and presidents. Yes, demanding that corporations end discrimination in hiring and business practices is always appropriate, but that's qualitatively different from making demands which are little more than shakedowns of companies that fear boycotts and bad publicity. Rather than spreading truth and hope, as Martin did, a new generation of African American leaders have emerged who seem to believe that they can succeed through the propagation of fear. The time may be different; the agenda may be different. But the method bears a chilling similarity to what Senator Joe McCarthy did when he claimed there were two commies in every garage and a pink chicken in the pot. Alas, there has so far been no Joseph Welch asking,

"At long last, have you no shame?" And instead of a Senate censure, there has so far been only capitulation from elected officials whose collective courage wouldn't fill John Hancock's inkwell.

"Life's most persistent and urgent question," Martin used to say, "is, 'What are you doing for others?'" His voice always rose to emphasize "for others."

Martin, I assure you, would be appalled at the behavior of some black leaders, pointing out that the role of a leader is, yes, to *lead*—that is, to guide others to a better place, a place worth going, not to keep them stagnant and hopeless by convincing them that they're powerless in a world that's been stacked against them solely because of their skin color. Martin never said or did anything that wasn't in some way a call to action and responsibility, believing that he could inspire even the worst of us to emulate the best of us. Watching these so-called leaders of today spreading despair in front of television cameras, he would shout out that they've got it all wrong. No, he'd say, the purpose of a leader is moral, not oral.

As early as 1956, in Montgomery, he understood clearly what it meant to lead, demonstrating that in both deed and word. He said, "Another thing that we must do in speeding up the coming of the new age is to develop intelligent, courageous, and dedicated leadership . . . leaders who avoid the extremes of 'hot-headedness' and 'Uncle Tomism' . . . leaders not in love with money, but in love with justice; leaders not in love with publicity, but in love with humanity; leaders who can subject their particular egos to the greatness of the cause."

Judged by these clear standards, few black leaders of today—at least the ones who have convinced enough people, especially the media, to call them "leader"—pass the Martin Luther King test of integrity. For them, money and publicity appear to trump justice, humanity is an abstraction with little connection to human beings, and the greatness of their egos often supersedes or obscures the righteousness of their cause. Those are the stark differences between men who seize opportunities and the man who heard a calling.

Over the last forty years I've been asked one question more than any other: Who now reminds me most of Martin Luther King. The answer is no one. Martin Luther King was sui generis—one of a kind, unique. Who, after all, is like Michelangelo? Or Galileo, or Einstein, or Mozart, or Shakespeare?

2

When you read biographies of extraordinary people it's striking how otherwise ordinary their childhoods generally seem to be. That would also be true of Martin Luther King, about whom it overstates the obvious to say that he was no ordinary man.

Even given his black skin and upbringing in Jim Crow Atlanta—where, for example, a law passed shortly before his birth in 1929 prohibited black barbers from cutting the hair of children under age 14—Martin enjoyed a mostly privileged upbringing; privileged, anyway, compared to most blacks. For that he could credit his maternal grandfather and his own father, two men whose stories of struggle, determination, and success stayed with him all his life.

His grandfather, A. D. (Adam Daniel) Williams, had become pastor of Ebenezer Baptist Church in 1894, nearly thirty years after its founding by a former slave, and turned it into one of Atlanta's most important black churches. Williams was fearless, determined not just to save souls in Jesus Christ but to see that this world here and now would be better after his time here. So he joined the NAACP as a charter member in 1909 and, when a local white newspaper printed derogatory remarks about the character of colored folk, the Reverend Williams led a boycott that eventually put the paper out of business. When a local bond issue for schools passed but without an allocation of monies for black schools, he organized rallies and fundraisers that helped build Washington High School, Atlanta's first high school for Negroes, who had been previously unable to matriculate past the ninth grade—a fact apparently lost on the white newspaper editor who'd ignorantly called them "ignorant."

No question, Reverend Williams was a force of nature. But if anything, Martin Luther King Sr. was even more powerful, considering what he'd overcome to be the father to the father of the modern civil rights movement.

"Daddy King," as he was later known, had been one of nine children born to sharecroppers in rural Georgia. He had a head for numbers that his own father lacked, so at age 12 he accompanied Dad on the day when annual accounts were settled up with the landowner whose cotton crop had been brought in by the Kings. Daddy knew that their landowner, like most, would cheat if he could, and sure enough Daddy reminded his father out loud, in front of the landowner, about reimbursement for the seed money, which wasn't listed on the settlement sheet. That infuriated the landowner, who did pay up, and for a night at least Daddy was a hero to his father. But the next day the landowner, still furious, showed up at the Kings' door and ordered them to clear out.

That was the beginning of the end for Daddy and his father, who began taking out his frustrations at being unable to care for his family *on* his family. How many other colored men were there like him under Jim Crow, men whose sense of desperation at being as powerless as children could find no outlet but violence? "Hey, boy!" would come the shouted salt on the wound.

One night when he was barely in his teens, Daddy stopped his father from beating anymore on his mother by beating on the old man, who in his anger threatened to kill him. His mother, fearing for her child's life, tearfully insisted that Daddy flee and begin making his way in the world. Alone at such a young age, his future didn't look bright; but at home, he might not have had even a single tomorrow.

Those were the days when church was the only place colored folk down South felt their separate accommodations were not inferior to the white man's. Taking refuge frequently in those confines, Martin Luther King Sr. found his calling at age 15 and became an itinerant minister, preaching in tiny rural churches for plate money and attracting something of a following. At 18, full of ambition, he showed up in Atlanta—and, compared with big-city sophisticates, immediately began feeling like an ignorant hick, someone whose lack of education showed every time he opened his mouth. Rather than complain about it, rather than return to the country, he returned to school.

At age 21.

Not high school—elementary school.

Think about that. Imagine the kind of determination and character it takes to sit in class learning the three Rs with children less than half your age.

After five years, working full-time as a driver, he graduated high school and set his sights on college. But Morehouse, the elite black university, believed he was too old at 27 to amount to much, and refused even to test him.

Daddy persevered, though. And when he was turned

down again, he stormed into the admissions office unin-
vited to make his best case. Whatever he said impressed
someone enough to admit him, and he repaid the favor by
graduating with distinction in four years.

He'd also impressed someone else—a woman. Pursuing her as single-mindedly and wholeheartedly as he had
his education, he impressed her enough to marry him, not
minding that everyone considered her well above his station in life. Her name was Alberta Williams, the daughter
of A. D. Williams. So when his father-in-law died suddenly
of a heart attack, Martin Luther King Sr. stepped into the
pulpit at Ebenezer Baptist Church.

Daddy and Alberta had three children: a girl, Christine;
a boy, Martin Jr.; and another boy, Alfred Daniel Williams
King. The children grew up during the Depression in a
kind of bubble created by their father's relative wealth as
the minister of a prosperous church whose attendance never
waned. They attended the high school that their grandfather had helped build and watched as their father worked to
ensure that teachers and facilities for blacks were every bit
as good as those on the other side of town.

Daddy King had high hopes for his first son, the one
whose temperament seemed preternaturally calm and fo-
cused. Not that he wasn't rebellious, though his rebellion
had more to do with embarrassment over the writhing,
Holy Roller nature of most black preachers, including his
father; Martin believed that the gospel could be delivered
in a compelling way without all the theatrics. And as for the
literalness of the Bible—well, to Martin the Good Book had
to be taken more symbolically than literally if the preacher
was going to establish his intellectual credibility and effect
change in *this* life. To him, before Kingdom Come there
was Kingdom Now.

Martin had choices in life—to be a lawyer, for example. But he'd felt the calling. And after graduating from Morehouse he enrolled at Crozer Theological Seminary in Pennsylvania (where he was voted president of his largely white class). Then, against his father's wish to have him return and join him at the pulpit at Ebenezer, he accepted a fellowship at Boston University for his Ph.D. Martin enjoyed himself in Boston; by accounts he was the most eligible black man in town—and the one who had the most fun. Then he met a beautiful and brilliant and talented singer named Coretta Scott, and pursued her, and married her—once again against his father's initial objections that he come home and wed the wealthiest young black woman in Atlanta, an heiress Daddy had had in mind for a long time.

As soon as he received his doctorate Martin grabbed his new bride—who'd grown up on a farm in Alabama but now preferred to stay in the North—and interviewed at Baptist churches in the South. He believed that his gospel of social change built on intellectual rigor and active nonviolence was as needed there as it would be effective. But, to his father's great disappointment, he would not be coming "home" to Ebenezer. He would not work in his father's shadow; he would not even work in the same state.

Martin applied at the Dexter Avenue Baptist Church in Montgomery, Alabama, where the city's Negro elite congregated to pray. After the interview came the audition—a Sunday in the pulpit.

By late that afternoon, the church deacons had made Martin the best-paid reverend in town, black or white. It would be a fateful decision for the nation and the world, one seemingly inconsequential at the time to anyone other than the young Kings, who now made their home in this strange city.

Barely a year later, Martin Luther King would find himself at the vortex of social forces more powerful than any in a hundred years. When Rosa Parks, tired after a long day as a department store seamstress, bravely refused to give up her seat on a Montgomery city bus and was arrested (three other blacks in the same row did get up and move to the back when the white driver threatened them), America's second revolution began in earnest.

Edgar Nixon, a friend of Rosa Parks and the most militant Negro in a city whose Negroes seemed otherwise content to wait for their heavenly reward, led the battle charge by insisting that this become a test case of legal segregation in public facilities. He and Jo Ann Robinson, a professor of English who headed an organization of black professional women, decided that the catalyst would be a boycott of the city buses, whose vital revenues to the city coffers were provided largely by Negroes riding from their homes on the outskirts to their jobs in the center of town. This being winter, with temperatures in the thirties at night, the first challenge was in getting riders to adhere to the boycott by walking such long distances in the cold.

The second and far greater challenge was to overcome decades of inertia that had sucked the life force from too many black people and left them assuming that change was what happened elsewhere, to others.

Montgomery's Negroes had long been divided into competing factions, and the possibility of the boycott holding seemed doubtful. For example, Martin's predecessor at Dexter Avenue Baptist had recently been insulted by a driver on a bus filled only with other blacks, many of whom were his congregants, but none of whom would go with him when he suggested that they protest the racist insult by exiting the bus.

To the surprise of many, the boycott held the first day, a Monday. But would it continue? Only if the city's Negroes could be persuaded that finally—finally!—their courage would not be spent in vain.

For those who believe in God, Martin has to be considered divinely sent; serendipity alone doesn't begin to justify the confluence of circumstances and events. New to town, he brought none of the baggage that hampered the city's longstanding black leaders—old hurts, old slights, old resentments. So when Edgar Nixon called a meeting to discuss tactics and strategy, Martin Luther King found himself in the right place at the right time with the right tools to deliver the right message for the right cause. He may not have even wanted what he got, but when fate called his name, he answered. The others, including Rev. Ralph Abernathy, named him president of the newly formed Montgomery Improvement Association. Which means he was assigned the job of making the boycott real—and making that reality worth the cost.

That night, as many as fifteen thousand black citizens of Montgomery crowded into, and onto the sidewalks around, Holt Street Baptist Church to hear Martin Luther King explain the boycott's purpose and its means: nonviolence.

The vast majority of people, of course, were hearing him for the first time, and after they did few doubted that life in Montgomery would ever be the same. He was interrupted countless times by roars of approval and stomping feet that created human thunder. No one had ever spoken that way before, and no one had ever said the things he said to them. And I like to think that if we, too, had been there—all of us—we, too, would have recognized this moment for what it was: the moment when everything changed and the better angels of America's nature were set to flight.

"And you know, my friends," Martin said, "there comes a time when people get tired of being trampled over by the iron feet of oppression. . .

"My friends, I want it to be known that we're going to work with grim and bold determination to gain justice. . . . And we are not wrong . . . in what we are doing. If we are wrong, the Supreme Court of this nation is wrong. If we are wrong, the Constitution of the United States is wrong. If we are wrong, God Almighty is wrong. If we are wrong, Jesus of Nazareth was merely a utopian dreamer that never came down to Earth. If we are wrong, justice is a lie, love has no meaning. And we are determined here in Montgomery to work and fight until justice runs down like water and righteousness like a mighty stream."

Amen.

No wonder our present-day self-proclaimed black leaders seem so diminished and wanting in comparison. And so self-serving.

3

"My call to the ministry," Martin wrote about himself as an 18-year-old, "was neither dramatic nor spectacular. It came neither by some miraculous vision nor by some blinding light of experience on the road to life. Moreover, it did not come as a sudden realization. Rather, it was a response to an inner urge that gradually came upon me. This urge expressed itself in a desire to serve God and humanity, and the feeling that my talent and my commitment could be expressed through the ministry. During my senior year in college . . . I came to see that God had placed a responsibility on my shoulders."

If Martin Luther King had not had that calling, well, the world would be too different to contemplate.

As he later told me, he believed that his rigorous academics had given him the ability to think clearly and critically, and that his grounding in seminary had provided enough intellectual ammunition for the sense of righteousness that imbued his ministry; it's what helped give him the courage to seize the moment in Montgomery—a moment that might never come again—not for him but for his people. And that, despite his relative lack of experience as compared to the other preachers, was what secured his leadership within the southern Negro community, allowing him to help found the Southern Christian Leadership Conference. No one who met him then, black or white, could fail to see that this young man was a born leader. The luck of the movement— and of all people who've benefited from a more just society, which means everyone—was that he'd been born black.

Martin excelled at developing programs and initiatives that served the needs of Negroes in communities where the SCLC had affiliates, and that effectiveness soon became a target for petty jealousies and rivalries that, in truth, dogged him through his days. Someone, it seems, is always trying to knock the great from their pedestals, even when the man on the pedestal wants to lift everyone else. Albany, Birmingham, the March on Washington—wherever Martin went, his growing popularity and fame were sometimes as much of a hindrance *inside* the Movement as they were a help *outside* the Movement, as his growing popularity and stature became a magnet for lesser men's envy. That only worsened after he won the Nobel Peace Prize in 1964.

Today, with the sharp edges of those events smoothed

by the decades, a simplistic narrative of that long-ago time seems to have emerged. It says that, compared to more militant blacks like Malcolm X and the Black Panthers, Martin Luther King was the white man's Negro leader—the man who considered violence immoral, stupid, and ultimately self-defeating. "Nonviolence is the answer to the crucial political and moral question of our time," he said in his Nobel acceptance speech, "the need for man to overcome oppression and violence without resorting to violence and oppression."

Martin was no establishment Negro, going along to get along. When it came to challenging the federal government's actions or inactions, that label at the time more aptly applied to the "mainstream" civil rights organizations like the NAACP (except for the leaders of its Legal Education Fund), the National Urban League, and the National Baptist Convention, all of whose leaders were more inclined to go along in order to get along with the Kennedy and Johnson administrations' deliberate pace on civil rights. Leaders of the Urban League and the National Urban League often received appointments in those administrations, or were invited onto corporate boards, or became trustees of foundations and universities. As a consequence of the generation gap and Martin's quick rise, some of them would refer to him derisively as "de Lawd."

Even so, none of them ever seriously questioned the integrity of his commitment to the struggle against injustice or the courage of his leadership; nor was he ever seriously accused of doing what he did for self-aggrandizement—unless, of course, the accuser was projecting his own motives onto Martin.

The envy never surprised Martin, nor threw him off track. As he once explained to me, "If you know your Bible, there's nothing about people that shocks you. Sometimes the ones who stand to gain the most by cooperating are the least cooperative."

James Baldwin summed up Martin well as early as 1961, when he wrote that Martin was "the first Negro leader in my experience, or the first in many generations," who says to whites exactly what he says to blacks, and speaks to both in the same cadence. "Most of his predecessors were in the extraordinary position of saying to white men, *Hurry,* while saying to black men, *Wait.*" No wonder whites, too, saw him as a leader and began following.

"The power of his personality and force of his beliefs have added dimension to our ferocious struggle," Baldwin wrote. "He has succeeded, in a way no Negro before him has managed to do, to carry the battle into the individual heart and make resolution the providence of the individual will. He has made it a matter, on both sides of the racial fence, of self-examination; and has incurred, therefore, the grave responsibility to continue to lead in the path that he has encouraged so many people to follow."

The operative word was "lead." Martin had become the commander of a righteous army that included all human beings, not just blacks. He actually believed that the subjugation of Negroes by whites was as damning to the souls of whites as it was harmful to blacks. What gave him moral authority and marked him as great was that he never asked, never encouraged, never even suggested that someone else engage in a battle that he himself was not prepared to lead personally. Time and again, even when the authorities offered him an alternative, he subjected himself to the risks and dangers of jail—and back then, jailers weren't constrained by video cameras, and those in the South were too frequently unconstrained by scruples.

Civil disobedience, Martin insisted, required consequences that ought to be borne by the disobedient. If no consequences follow, then there's no point to the act because only such consequences born by the disobedient illustrate the law's immorality and arouse the public. (Contrast this with young, mostly white college students of the era who frequently bullied their way into the administration building, trashed everything in sight, and then presented the dean or school president with a list of demands, the first of which was always "no reprisals.")

During his Montgomery speech in 1956 Martin quoted the Civil War–era poet Josiah Holland: "God give us men. A time like this demands strong minds, great hearts, true faith, and ready hands; men whom the lust of office cannot buy; men who will not lie; men who stand before a demagogue and damn his treacherous flatteries without winking; tall men, sun-crowned, who live above the fog; in public duty and private thinking."

God giveth, and God taketh away. He may have given and taken Martin Luther King from us, but He has not replaced him since. I think even Martin, in all his humility, would have to agree. At the least, he'd be saddened by the men who claim his place.

4

September 2007. Demonstrators, possibly as many as 50,000, have crowded into the central Louisiana town of Jena, population 3,000, to protest the criminal justice system's treatment of several black high school students—the "Jena Six," they've been nicknamed—who'd been charged with attempted murder after beating a white student unconscious. The charges had since been reduced, but backstory is important.

A year before, a black student asked the principal whether he was allowed to sit under that tree over there, and the principal told him he could sit wherever he damn well pleased. But that tree over there, by racist tradition, had always provided shade for whites only. And the whites didn't like any blacks sitting there. So the next day after that student and some friends went over to chat with some white classmates, three other white boys sent a clear message, hanging nooses from a bough.

Like swastikas to Jews, nooses to southern blacks are a terrifying and agonizing sight, one that invokes the kind of history that's supposed to remain in the past, not become a current event. The principal tried expelling the white boys who'd dangled the nooses, but the school board overrode him and gave them only a three-day suspension. Meanwhile, the district attorney reportedly looked for something more heinous to charge them with and found nothing on the Louisiana books about hanging nooses, even though the boys' intent was clearly vile. The boys soon returned to school with the sense that they'd gotten away with it, their actions condoned.

Racial tensions at school became inflamed. Over the next few months several fights broke out between blacks and whites, culminating with a group of six black male students attacking a white student who'd had nothing to do with the nooses. They jumped him from behind and cold-cocked him before stomping on him. The beating was severe enough that the district attorney (over)charged all six with attempted second-degree murder, though the charges were later reduced and all but the most vicious, Mychal Bell (who'd apparently stood on the beaten boy's head), were released on bail. In June, Bell was convicted of second-degree battery by an all-white jury. But his conviction was overturned by the Third Circuit Court of Appeals, which ruled that the 17-year-old—16 at the time of the attack—should not have been tried as an adult. Even so, the D.A. kept him in jail another week while deciding whether to file charges in juvenile court. And when he did, the judge agreed to release him on bond.

By then, my brothers Jesse Jackson and Al Sharpton, America's two most famous "black leaders," had shown up in Jena with a contingent of other celebrities, including Martin Luther King III, to lead a protest against the over-zealous charges originally filed against the black youths. As Stefanie Brown, the 26-year-old national youth direc-tor of the NAACP, told the Associated Press, "It's not just about Jena, but about inequalities and disparities around the country."

Another 26-year-old, a black Jena resident, told the *New York Times*, "There's always been prejudice and bigotry here. Every day they're throwing away a black man's life down here."

What are the leaders and demonstrators demanding with their chants, speeches, placards? "Free the Jena Six."

The original indictments of the six black students, as well as the continued incarceration of the sixth even after the court overturned his conviction, does indeed indicate the persistence of racism in the justice system. One has to ask whether six white students in Jena would be charged with aggravated assault and attempted murder for beating a black student who went home after treatment? Would a white 17-year-old in Jena be tried as an adult and convicted, then held in jail after the conviction is voided by a higher court? Is there a glaring double standard in the justice sys-tem, one punishment for whites and one for blacks?

These are serious questions worthy of investigation, and a

search for their answers leads quite properly to wonder what Martin Luther King would say about the situation in Jena.

I promise you, he would have abhorred everything but the peacefulness of the demonstration, starting with Jesse Jackson and Al Sharpton treating Mychal Bell like Rosa Parks; and he would've shrieked at the AP headline: "Louisiana Protests Hark Back to '50s, '60s."

Hark back to what? he would've asked. For Martin, Jena and the Jena Six would exemplify just how far the African American community down South and, more explicitly, our civil rights leadership nationally have strayed off course from the beliefs and precepts that guided Martin Luther King and therefore the movement four decades ago. At a time when the nation's streets are black killing fields—with blacks killing blacks by the dozens every week for no rational reason—the leadership appears concerned only with what might get on television; and apparently twenty more gangstas shot down last Saturday night is just another dog-bites-man, old-news story unworthy of a mention. If America's black leadership truly had black America's best interests in mind, *that's* the issue the leaders would address. Instead, they put on a circus, just like the Roman emperors did whenever they wanted to divert the plebs' attention.

Martin's goal was the establishment in American society, then the world, of a "beloved community," a term coined about fifty years before Martin died by the theologian Josiah Royce, founder of the Fellowship of Reconciliation. Martin joined that society and became its most famous proponent of peaceful conflict resolution. In his vision of a beloved community, the symbolic evil of hanging nooses would be met with nonviolent conflict resolution, not with hitting, kicking, and stomping.

But it's worse than that, as he would've learned in his

search for truth. A black U.S. attorney investigated the incident and concluded that not only did the beaten white student have nothing to do with hanging the nooses, but the beating itself had nothing to do with the noose incident; this was an unprovoked beating for beating's sake, delivered by thugs who felt they had license to do as they pleased. Only afterward, when the D.A. grossly overcharged the six with attempted murder, were the nooses raised as an issue in order to gain sympathy and devise a defense strategy. As for young Mr. Bell—he who was hailed by Jesse and Al, and visited personally by them in jail—at the time of the beating he was already on probation for a previous assault, one that had derailed his promising football career and a possible Division 1-A scholarship.

That's why the rallying cry heard before, during, and after the protest, "Free the Jena Six," would make Martin shake his head in sadness, as would the petition with tens of thousands of signatures demanding that authorities "drop all charges."

It's true that the town of Jena had twice voted overwhelmingly for the loathsome racist David Duke when he ran for U.S. senator and Louisiana governor in the 1990s. In fact, so had most whites in Louisiana (where more than 250 blacks had been lynched between Reconstruction and World War II). "But so what," Martin would've said. This was 2007. The Jena Six were not innocents, like the three civil rights volunteers who in 1965 had gone to march for voting rights in Selma, Alabama, and were murdered by white racists. The Jena Six were thugs of varying degrees. And the very notion of freeing violent young men and thereby absolving them of their crimes was anathema to his worldview. This man who gladly and willingly spent days, weeks, and months of his life in jails across the South for civilly violating immoral laws would hardly have countenanced letting the six off without appropriate punishment.

"Men and women," he said, "have a moral obligation to obey just and right laws. . . . It's wrong to be dishonest and unjust; it's wrong to use your brother as a means to an end; it's wrong to waste the precious life that God has given you in riotous living, it is eternally and absolutely wrong; it's wrong to hate, it always has been wrong and it always will be wrong."

Martin surely would've agreed with Ernest Hemingway's dispatch from Italy in 1923, soon after Benito Mussolini's new fascist party had taken control of the government by threat, intimidation, and brute force against the rival communists. The fascists, Hemingway wrote, "had a taste of unpenalized lawlessness, unpunished murder, and the right to riot when and where they pleased. So now they have become almost as great a danger to the peace of Italy as the Reds ever were."

What a shrewd and concise summation of "unpenalized lawlessness" and "unpunished murder," its truth confirmed irrefutably by history.

Being jailed to protest immorality and being freed for committing immorality are as different as right and wrong.

"One who breaks an unjust law," Martin said, referring to a law imposed by the majority on the minority without imposing it on itself, "must do it openly, lovingly, and with a willingness to accept the penalty by staying in jail to arouse the conscience of the community over its injustice."

For this protest in Jena to hark back appropriately to the 1950s and 1960s, the Jena Six would have to have been arrested for refusing not to sit under the white tree.

In Martin's time and on his watch, the Jena Six would

never have been celebrated for committing violence against their brother—yes, their brother, be he white or black.

In Martin's time, violent thugs were never to be made a cause célèbre, even if the underlying issue—double standards in the justice system—was otherwise worthy of scrutiny.

And what Martin would tell these young men today is to pay for their crimes by doing a just amount of time.

The Jena Six, after all, are hardly the Scottsboro boys—nine innocent black teens accused of raping two white women in Alabama. Their guilt as perpetrators of violence was never in doubt. Indeed, Mr. Bell's attorney was himself black; he called no witnesses on Bell's behalf, and they faced an all-white jury when no black citizens of Jena bothered to respond to the jury summonses.

Anyone who compares Jena to Montgomery and Selma, for example, demeans both himself and the memories of those who changed the world by striking in Montgomery so that public accommodations could be truly public, and by marching to Selma under threat of state-sanctioned violence so that Negroes could register to vote without paying poll taxes or passing literacy tests.

Civil rights became the Civil Rights Movement in Montgomery not just because the bus strike succeeded; the Movement began there and created a magnetic pull because of *how* the strike succeeded. It succeeded exactly as Martin had imagined it might ever since he grasped that Gandhi's passive resistance techniques were not passivity in the face of evil but rather nonviolent resistance to it that works by shining a moral spotlight on the act and the actor.

For a year, Montgomery's Negroes boycotted the city's buses at huge inconvenience to themselves and their livelihoods, and risked beatings or worse by frustrated whites—but they were joyful, unified by the moral superiority they demonstrated every day through their peaceful resistance.

In the past, most southern Negroes had been afraid to confront the white power structure and were content to wait until they died to become equal. Now, in Montgomery, nonviolence was the glue that held them together and, with each passing day, ennobled them to themselves and to each other. As importantly, it also humanized them to the nation that watched them on television and decided, a few Americans at a time, that the dignity being demonstrated was something worth aspiring to.

On the day the strike finally ended, Martin boarded a city bus near his home. "I believe you're Reverend King," the white driver said to him. "Glad to have you with us this morning."

Any correlation between Montgomery and Jena is strictly fictional, and unintentionally confirms the truth of Martin's observation that "the only sin for the average modern man is to disobey the Eleventh Commandment: 'Thou shalt not get caught.' . . . This attitude has led to a philosophy of the survival of the slickest. . . ."

Were he here now, Martin would seek an answer to whether justice is yet equal by race in Jena, and he'd do everything possible to rectify any inequities. But I'm quite sure that first he'd have some other penetrating questions, starting with the parents of the six black students: What kind of leaders were they to their own children? How did they raise the boys? What rules of moral conduct did they instill? Were they themselves good examples to their sons? Did they insist on a commitment to excellence, especially in education, and teach their boys that a thousand David Dukes are no match for a brain harnessed by self-discipline and desire? Have they themselves condemned their children's violence? And how much of the Movement's real struggle from the past did they pass on, so that their kids would know of sacrifices their forebears had made for them—as well as the differences between an arrest for beating up someone and an arrest for nonviolently violating an unjust law?

When he was finished with the young men's parents, Martin would call out the black leaders who either organized the protest or showed up to capitalize on it—and he'd reserve his most biting sermon for them.

To Martin, they'd have the most to answer for.

5

In the spring of 2006, three white members of the Duke University lacrosse team were charged with raping and assaulting a black woman who'd been hired to perform the previous month as a stripper at a team party. She claimed that more than one member had brutalized her, beaten her, and even sodomized her with a broomstick.

There was outrage not just in Durham but around the country. Soon, though, credibility questions began clouding her story—rather, stories, which kept changing, as did the testimony of a second stripper who the first young woman had insisted was also beaten.

Even so, the white district attorney, behind in the polls before his upcoming reelection campaign in predominantly black Durham, pressed ahead in what many North Carolinians must've recognized as a lynch-mob atmosphere—"Give 'em a fair trial, then hang 'em."

(Eventually, so many problems were to emerge with the accuser and the case that the charges would be dropped, the boys declared innocent, and the D.A. forced to resign and stripped of his law license.)

It was regrettable when Jesse Jackson, Al Sharpton, and some of the country's other black leaders and celebrities proclaimed the white boys guilty and pronounced the black accuser a pitiable victim of historic injustice—the kind that was supposed to have disappeared long ago. They were joined by mostly white Duke professors and America's most powerful media outlets, including and especially the *New York Times*. So the very same people who in the past had urged against a rush to judgment in other criminal matters—for instance, O. J. Simpson's arrest for a double murder on a mountain of physical evidence—now galloped toward judgment. And why not? The Durham incident was too perfect a page from the standard narrative of race, class, and sex—black oppressed versus white oppressor—that forms the script from which tens of millions apparently recite without a second thought, as if mindlessly reeling off the words to "Three Blind Mice." And the usual suspects refused to take less than leading roles.

"Black women; white men," Rev. Jackson wrote. "A stripper; and a team blowout. The wealthy white athletes—many from prep schools—of Duke; and the working-class woman from historically black North Carolina Central. Race and class and sex. What happened? We don't know for sure because the Duke players are maintaining a code of silence."

A code of silence, he alleged, like police who circle the wagons around one of their own, or white racists who conspire beneath hoods of anonymity. Here, the silence of innocence was mistakenly interpreted by Jesse and some others as ipso facto proof of guilt.

To be charitable, this was appallingly disingenuous.

"We know," he continued, "that the two girls were abused."

We do? The possibility that they might not have been—a possibility raised by the second young woman herself—or that the accused might be innocent would not and could not be considered by Jackson in this charged atmosphere. How do we know that? Because he offered to pay the alleged victim's college tuition out of his own pocket *after* the first DNA tests came back from the lab and implicated not a single member of the team.

By then, though, facts had ceased to be important. All that mattered now was that the standard narrative continue to be the thrilling campfire story told every day to prove that the legacy of white slave owners raping their female slaves had not disappeared into history. All that mattered now was to reestablish exalted victim status not just for the victim but for our race.

To Martin, victims were those who refused to do for themselves when they were in a position to do so. To many current black leaders, victimhood is that thing devoutly to be pursued and legitimized. How unfortunate. The great burden of leadership carries both celebrity and public responsibility, and the exercise of that responsibility can often be difficult, particularly when it threatens a leader's acceptance and popularity among his immediate supporters and broader constituency. The history of our movement indicates that regrettably, my friend and brother Jesse Jackson has not always applied the precepts and principles consistent with how he was guided and mentored as a courageous disciple of Martin Luther King.

For example, some years ago, in Decatur, Illinois, Jesse championed the case of seven high school students—gang members—who'd been suspended by the school board for two years after fighting in the stands at a school football game. Video of the brawl demonstrates how violently they acted, without regard for anyone's safety, and expulsion as well as prosecution might not have been inappropriate. Jesse injected himself into the proceedings and argued for their reinstatement, comparing the young men's struggle to both Martin Luther King and Nelson Mandela.

This was an exaggeration at best, no matter how well intended, and it had the effect of squandering his own moral capital and credibility, as well as demeaning the contribution and sacrifice of both Martin and Mandela.

Rather than use these young men as a negative example and insist that others take their educations seriously and strive for excellence, which is what Martin would have counseled, Jesse overlooked the fact that three of them were repeating their freshman year for *the third time*, and that together the six (one withdrew from school) had missed an aggregate 350 days of classes.

What would Martin say? He'd say, "Brother Jesse, what you're doing by running to the spotlight defending these particular young men is sending a message that everything is copasetic—because if these boys represent the biggest problems black people have in America, the struggle must surely be over. Think about it."

As for our brilliant and talented Reverend Al, there are also some constructive lessons to be gleaned from the way he applied his leadership skills to the Duke lacrosse team case.

A public figure's public mistakes, incomplete or absent apologies, and improperly explained actions eventually make true leadership far more difficult, if not impossible. This, I think, has been the case with Al Sharpton. Sharpton's leadership baggage as regards his involvement in the Duke case began with the Tawana Brawley incident in which a 15-year-old black girl falsely accused white men of rape and smearing feces on her. (An investigative report requested by then–New York governor Mario Cuomo concluded that the incident had been a complete hoax.) The baggage then accrued further, dragging down some of his otherwise courageous and moral actions, by the evidence that he either led or instigated two anti-Jewish demonstrations in New York (one in Crown Heights, the other in Harlem), which together resulted in the deaths of eight. By the time Al encouraged the asinine shock jock Don Imus to ask for *his*—Sharpton's—forgiveness, when the forgiveness Imus should've sought was directly from the young black women on Rutgers' basketball team he'd offended with his "nappy-headed 'hos" comment, Al's actions were seen merely as comical and ironic. Months before then, after all, he had already waded hip-deep into the Duke situation by hinting not so subtly that unless charges were filed by the Durham D.A. against the supposed perps on the lacrosse team, there might be a little trouble in the streets—you know, "no justice, no peace." And then he'd offered to join Jackson in picking up the tab for the young woman's education.

What would Martin say? He'd say, "Brother Al, you have a responsibility not to wrap the mantle of the moral legitimacy of our struggle around causes and persons that corrupt and dishonor the sacrifices and legacy of our civil rights struggle."

Perhaps saddest of all, though, was the performance of the NAACP.

For nearly a hundred years the group that had done so much excellent work on behalf of blacks falsely accused of everything from jaywalking to murder revealed itself to be—not for the first time—little more than a credulous cheerleader for any team so long as it wears the color black.

In the past, justice meant fairness to "the nation's oldest

and largest civil rights organization." Now, justice appears to have become merely an accidental outcome instead of a bedrock principle; it now means that *all* black defendants who've committed crimes against whites are to be freed, and all black plaintiffs are beyond reproach, regardless of their credibility. From O. J. Simpson's alleged double murder to Michael Jackson's alleged child abuse to Michael Vick's animal abuse, the NAACP frequently leads the charge to inject race into cases where the content of the defendants' character is clearly more of a factor than the color of their skin. (Ironies abound with the efforts to racialize the prosecutions of Simpson, a man who preferred to think of himself as a wealthy white, and Michael Jackson, who's tried for more than twenty years to turn himself—literally—into a white man.)

The association even took up the cause, in 2007, of a black Los Angeles firefighter named Tennie Pierce, nineteen years on the force, who sued the department and the city on racial grounds when a Latino paramedic on his team played a practical joke by putting dog food in his spaghetti. Facts and context did not discourage the local NAACP office from its insistence that Pierce had been the victim of a viciously racist prank.

In truth, Pierce himself, all 6 feet 5 inches of him, had long been known as a prankster among the LAFD's renowned pranksters. Photographs of him leading more, shall we say, physically assertive pranks confirmed testimony given by other firefighters—black, white, brown, and yellow—with whom he'd always gotten along well and earned a reputation for affability and athleticism. The day before the incident, during a volleyball game, Pierce had repeatedly made fun of his nearly foot shorter Latino colleague ("I take craps bigger than you") while demanding that his teammates get him the ball so he could spike it. "Feed the big dog," he shouted. "Feed the big dog."

Well, the big dog ate, all right. And then he fumed, and then he dissembled, claiming at a tearful press conference months later, as NAACP reps stood behind him, that after unwittingly swallowing the food he'd been taunted by nine laughing firefighters, all white. In fact, the firefighters numbered eight and were a mix of races and ethinicities. No matter. The city eventually paid Pierce $1.5 million from its coffers and thereby sent a message to employers, private and public, that blacks potentially view all incidents as racial—so beware before hiring.

In Durham, the North Carolina NAACP's general counsel posted a list of eighty-three "Crimes and Torts committed by Duke Lacrosse Team Players" on its website, even though he could prove none of them. Spokesmen for the group joined with the corrupt white D.A., Mike Nifong, to call for indictments and punishments based on the inferences of class and race, spreading more lies and innuendo about the accused players. Then, when questions about the accuser's story began to accumulate into an unavoidable pile, the NAACP called for a gag order—a legal tactic used in the past to silence innocent black defendants. And even after Nifong was forced to drop the rape charges and hand the case over to the state attorney general's office, the chapter's president said that this "could potentially have a chilling effect on women, particularly African Americans, filing sexual violence complaints." It did not, apparently, occur to him that false allegations have a far more chilling effect on innocents by raising doubt in juries' minds about truly guilty defendants.

At last, when the case's final threads had unraveled, the head of the NAACP chapter declared that the issues of "classism, racism, and sexual violence" would still have to be addressed, "regardless of where this particular case goes. We have to face that truth, whatever it is."

If only.

6

If only truth were the intention.

If only the current crop of civil rights leaders understood that crying wolf—or supporting those who do—only hurts the people it's theoretically intended to help.

If only the current crop of civil rights leaders could see how much damage they do to the cause of justice—real justice—and race relations by foolishly asserting, in essence, that this is still 1913 and that most blacks in the early twenty-first century had not achieved at least middle-class status through their own hard work and determination, with the top 20 percent of earners becoming the fastest-growing segment. How belittling.

What would Martin say? He'd repeat what he said, and wrote, after the expression "Black Power" came into vogue and became associated with the use of bloodshed and separatism: "The slogan was an unwise choice at the outset. With the violent connotations that now attach to the words it has become dangerous and injurious. I have made it clear that for the SCLC and me, adherence to nonviolence and Negro-white unity is an imperative. Our method is related to our objective. We have never sought the moral goal of freedom and equality by immoral means. Black supremacy or aggressive black violence is as invested with evil as white supremacy or white violence."

Amen.

Yes, of course, we still have a ways to go. But by walking backward, all we see is the past. When leaders declare at the Jena Six demonstration that "there are more black men in jail than in college," they perpetuate a well-established myth—one that's been echoed ad nauseum, like a mantra, by the so-called black leadership. In fact, I myself used to restate this myth in some of my public speeches until I decided to do my own investigative research. I regret the mistake and what it implies, that blacks are an inferior race morally, intellectually, and spiritually.

Indeed, this misinformation also reaches the ears of white America, so it infects their view, too, of blacks and black accomplishment; and in that way the whole sick circle continues to feed the stereotypical views which the media are all too glad to purvey as fact, even if it's done through the gauze-covered lens of white guilt. No wonder at a Democratic presidential debate candidate John Edwards, a former senator—from the southern state of North Carolina—said that, if we keep putting black criminals in prison, there'll be so many "pretty soon we're not going to have a young African American male population in America. They're all going to be in prison or dead. One of the two." No one corrected him, not that night nor the next day in ordinary media coverage of the event.

Reporters under the spell of political correctness hurry to black leaders for a confirming comment about what they already believe, that life for blacks can never be fair or good so long as whites hold majority power; and then they broadcast the story as they know it to be true. In logic, that's called a tautology. The more it's told, the truer it becomes for those telling it, making it harder to question the narrative next time. (See: Nazis and the Big Lie.) Which of the elite black spokesmen whose fame and fortune are created by white cameras have the nerve and political courage to suggest that sometimes, even just sometimes, blacks are the masters of their own fates and not persecuted by the Great White Bigot? That would be akin to a cow applying for work in a butcher shop.

For the record—and attention, Senator Edwards—according to the 2005 Census, 864,000 black men were attending college in this country, while 802,000 were incarcerated in federal and state prisons and local jails; which means there was an enrollment "surplus" of black men in college. (More than 2 million black women, by the way, attend college.)

It seems silly to have to point out that that's good news, not bad news. But the good news gets even better: black men of traditional college age—that is, 18 to 24—are four times as likely to be in college as locked up.

Unless you're invested in black inferiority, this is news worthy of at least toasting, if not celebrating, as is the American Council on Education's report that African Americans are 56 percent more likely to attend college than we were just twenty years ago. (There is, however, a legitimate issue to be debated, and that is the declining ratio of black men to black women in our colleges and universities. On the other hand, this isn't solely a black issue, since the same trend applies to whites.)

These figures likely come as a revelation to anyone whose worldview is defined by America's self-proclaimed black leaders or their abettors in the mainstream press. That's why a 40-something African American filmmaker named Janks Morton produced a documentary in 2007 titled *What Black Men Think*. And what they think about themselves, he discovered, is often absurdly wrong. For that, he blames the government, the media, and present black leadership for conspiring to stick with the clichéd narrative either out of intellectual laziness or for their own aggrandizement.

When asked by a *Washington Post* reporter writing about the documentary whether he knew the true numbers of blacks in college, a spokesman for the national NAACP said he remembered once hearing the data but hadn't looked into the matter since; and anyway, "we still are not where we need to be, and that causes rifts in our community in a number of ways."

You see how it works? As the Inquisition said to Galileo, we don't need no stinkin' facts. However much better things are, they'll never be good enough to be declared good by the current black leadership (with some notable exceptions). Never. Because if they were, then there'd be no reason for blacks to have black leaders. (When was the last time you heard the phrase "white leader"?) And, after all, "black leader" isn't exactly an eye-catcher atop a résumé for anyone who suddenly finds himself unemployed after enough blacks *and* whites hear the truth about race relations. Today, many black leaders work full-time to convince their constituents that whites are right now conspiring to step on their throats, and that the only thing between them and destitution is the current leadership out there "fighting for you."

Black victimhood sells, and black leaders market it as a commodity, like sugar and shoes. But who sees the terrible, colossal irony perpetrated by these leaders, many of them clergy, who would never consider themselves to be Toms? Victimhood as exalted is actually the identical message peddled by those Jim Crow–era Negro preachers who counseled patience and promised equality after death.

What modern leaders offer is no better: an ever-refracting racial prism that explains to Tyrone why he doesn't drive a Rolls and to Kanisha why she doesn't live in a McMansion? The miracle is that Kanisha and Tyrone, beaten down by such messages of hopelessness, even bother to get out of bed in the morning. Eisenhower warned of the military-industrial complex. Today, Martin would warn of the complex victim industry whose self-interest lies in not telling blacks that they control—and choose—their own fates through their own actions. At least during Jim Crow, churchgoers believed that a better day was coming.

Martin would not question the courage of today's black leaders, but he might very well wonder about their dedication to the cause that would be furthered, if not achieved, by an insistence that black people avoid the quicksand of victimization and instead pursue excellence regardless of barriers. In the twenty-first century, moral leadership requires recognition that our worldwide economy is based on information, and that knowledge and the content of someone's character are clearly far more important than skin color. Let our black leadership lead by developing programs, strategies, and tactics that help our young people commit themselves to excellence.

And if they want to see an example of the cruel monster they've created, they can look not at Tyrone and Kanisha but at a self-made black millionaire who still believes the white bogeyman is out to get him. On national television, Philadelphia Eagles quarterback Donovan McNabb insisted with a straight face that black quarterbacks face more pressure, scrutiny, and criticism than do white quarterbacks.

I'd like to introduce Mr. McNabb to Doug Williams, a black quarterback from Grambling College who began his NFL career in the 1970s with the new Tampa Bay Buccaneers. On a daily basis he heard fans, other players, reporters, and management question the innate abilities of a black quarterback. But Doug became the best quarterback in the short and miserable history of Tampa Bay, leaving after several seasons and skipping to the short-lived United States Football

League. He then returned to the NFL's Washington Red-
skins, where he encountered the same questions, concerns,
and doubts about the abilities of a black quarterback and
led the Skins to a 42–10 rout of the Denver Broncos in
Super Bowl XXII. Not only was he named the game's Most
Valuable Player, but it should be noted that the losing quarterback was the very white, and very talented, John Elway.

Donovan may also want to talk to Warren Moon. He
was a gifted quarterback at the University of Washington,
where he beat a favored University of Michigan team in the
Rose Bowl and won the game's MVP honors. But no NFL
team bothered to draft him. So he went to Canada—the
CFL—playing six seasons and winning five consecutive
league championships. At last the NFL came knocking, and
in the final nine years of his career, he managed to finish
third all-time in passing yardage and made nine Pro Bowl
appearances. Imagine the kinds of records he would've set
had he not been the victim of such obvious racism. Even
so, Warren Moon never uttered a discouraging word, never
wondered aloud what might have been if.

Poor Donovan McNabb. He heard raspberries from Philadelphia fans—who are well known for booing every one of
their professional athletes when they fail in the clutch, including Hall of Fame legends Mike Schmidt and Julius Erv-
ing; hell, they even once booed Santa Claus—and concluded
that their displeasure with him had something to do with
skin color. That's how absurd this has become. Of course,
a year before, when (black) wide receiver Terrell Owens was
still his teammate and suggested that the Eagles would be
better with Brett Favre—the white Green Bay Packers quarterback—McNabb pulled a play out of the race victims' play-
book and called the comment "black-on-black crime."

I wonder what he'd think about my friend who's white,

short, middle-aged, and maybe a little paunchy—no one's idea of someone to fear physically. Yet he tells me that every time he gets into an elevator alone with a strange woman, she clutches her purse tightly and fear glints in her eyes behind a fake smile. Since he's not black, he laments, he has to blame her reaction on his gender instead of his color.

I don't have to wonder what Martin would say. He'd say that promoting every issue in which a black and a white are on opposite sides as another example of racism only encourages defeatism and self-loathing among blacks who don't know any better, as well as cry-wolf indifference to real racism among whites. He'd say that wallowing in victimhood is a guarantee you won't pursue excellence.

And he'd say, "Brother Donovan, can't you sit there with your millions of dollars in salary and millions more from corporate sponsorships that you get because so many millions of whites admire you, and think of something else to complain about? If you want the boos to stop, shut up about your color, hit the open receiver, scramble for a first down, and win the Super Bowl. And if you want to hear real booing and have to fend off real tomatoes, go to Chicago and trade places with whoever's throwing the ball for the Bears. See if Rex Grossman's still around."

THREE

WHAT WOULD MARTIN SAY ABOUT AFFIRMATIVE ACTION?

MARTIN LUTHER KING WOULD NOT UNDERSTAND the term "affirmative action" the way we use it today. No wonder. The words were first used by President Kennedy, two months into his presidency, when he signed an executive order that created the Committee on Equal Employment Opportunity in order to legally prohibit racial discrimination on projects funded by federal monies. It seems so obvious now that feeding bigots at the public trough isn't kosher, we can be forgiven for not remembering, or knowing, what a big step forward the order appeared to be at the time.

Maybe that's because the first prohibition against discriminatory hiring policies had come during World War II, when President Roosevelt, at the urging of his wife, Eleanor, and in order to head off a planned march on Washington organized by A. Philip Randolph, signed an executive order establishing the Fair Employment Practices Committee. Defense contractors responsible for supplying the "arsenal of democracy" suddenly had to hire far more blacks, particularly in skilled positions. And that was good. But as soon as the war ended, white soldiers returning from overseas began taking their jobs back, and without a federal enforcement agency guarding against a restoration of the status quo, it would be another fifteen years till JFK forbade again what had briefly been forbidden before.

No one could possibly have predicted that the young president's use of the phrase "affirmative action," removed from the executive order's original context, would soon lie at the heart of one of America's most divisive debates.

Three years after that directive, Congress passed and President Lyndon Johnson signed into law the Civil Rights Act of 1964, which raised the bar on tolerable discrimination even higher, as did the subsequent Voting Rights Act of 1965.

Then came an executive order by LBJ requiring government contractors "to take affirmative action" toward minority job applicants, which meant that the employers had to leave a paper trail showing that they'd at least tried to hire qualified blacks. There were exploitable loopholes, of course, but now we seemed to be getting somewhere, if only by baby steps.

And where we seemed to be getting was outlined by LBJ in his commencement speech to the Howard University class of '65. He said, "You do not wipe away the scars of centuries by saying: 'Now, you are free to go where you want, do as you desire, and choose the leaders you please.' You do not take a man who for years has been hobbled by chains, liberate him, bring him to the starting line of a race, saying, 'You are free to compete with all the others,' and still justly believe you have been completely fair. . . . This is the next and more profound stage of the battle for civil rights. We seek not just freedom but opportunity; not just legal equity but human ability; not just equality as a right and a theory, but equality as a fact and as a result."

These were powerful words, especially from a child of Texas—words that hinted tantalizingly at an apology with teeth—that is, action. And as far as Martin Luther King was concerned, they echoed his own words from his most celebrated speech. Delivered in front of hundreds of thousands as a culmination to the historic March on Washington at the end of August 1963, the "I Have a Dream" speech had spent the first several paragraphs essentially saying the same thing.

Here are two of those paragraphs:

"In a sense we've come to our nation's capital to cash a check. When the architects of our republic wrote the magnificent words of the Constitution and the Declaration of Independence, they were signing a promissory note to which every American was to fall heir. This note was a promise that all men, yes, black men as well as white men, would be guaranteed the 'unalienable Rights' of 'Life, Liberty and the pursuit of Happiness.' It is obvious today that America has defaulted on this promissory note, insofar as her citizens of color are concerned. Instead of honoring this sacred obligation, America has given the Negro people a bad check, a check which has come back marked 'insufficient funds.'

"But we refuse to believe that the bank of justice is bankrupt. We refuse to believe that there are insufficient funds in the great vaults of opportunity of this nation. And so, we've come to cash this check, a check that will give us upon demand the riches of freedom and the security of justice."

The language may have been different from LBJ's, but the sentiments are comparable. I know that because I wrote Martin's words, in constant consultation with him, during the weeks he and his family stayed at my house in New York before the March on Washington (which is, by the way, when the FBI first started tapping my phones—and got the idea to tap *his* phones based on what was heard).

For Martin, the issue was how best and quickest to right a historical injustice whose ramifications were still being felt across black America. He was committed to the concept of fairness, and at the time achieving that level playing field we speak of today looked like it needed to take the form of financial reparations—immediate payment of a debt to make its recipients whole. Nothing less seemed moral, and nothing later than now seemed acceptable. Promises of future promises wouldn't get it done.

An interviewer for *Playboy* asked Martin whether it was true that he felt Negroes deserved a "multibillion-dollar program of preferential treatment."

Martin explained that no "fair-minded citizen" could deny that the black man had been deprived, robbed, enslaved, and denied the right to earn a living. He said, "All of America's wealth today could not adequately compensate its Negroes for his centuries of exploitation and humiliation."

Before the 1964 Republican National Convention, Stanley Levison and I helped prepare Martin's remarks for presentation to the Platform Committee. That may sound strange now, presenting a potential plank for reparations to Republicans, but at the time it made proper sense. Those were the days when blacks had not yet begun to vote reflexively for Democrats and were more likely to remember that Lincoln had been a Republican. Indeed, it was President Dwight Eisenhower, a Republican, who surprised the nation in general and Arkansas in particular when he sent in the 101st Airborne to escort nine black students inside Central High School in Little Rock.

In Martin's speech to the committee, he cannily noted that the enactment of the GI Bill twenty years before was intended to compensate our soldiers who'd been "deprived of certain advantages and opportunities" while away at war. The generous package of veteran's benefits, significantly called a "Bill of Rights," included educational subsidies, living expenses, concessions to buy homes with little or no money down and at lower interest rates, low rates for small-business loans, and a leg up in the stiff competition for civil service jobs. In other words, all of society was required to take affirmative action on behalf of veterans. And why not? Preferential treatment and employment were logical ways of "compensating the veteran for his time lost in school or in his career or in business."

But, as Martin wrote in *Why We Can't Wait*, the sacrifices of Negroes first as slaves and then as lowly paid human mules were rarely recognized. While the country stood firmly in support of well-deserved perks for vets, "Few people considered the fact that, in addition to being enslaved for two centuries, the Negro was, during all these years, robbed of the wages of his toil. . . . Yet, a price can be placed on unpaid wages. . . . The payment should be in the form of a massive program by the government of special, compensatory measures which could be regarded as a settlement in accordance with the accepted practice of common law."

It should go without saying that the Republican convention did not adopt a reparations plank in its platform—not that it would've mattered anyway with Barry Goldwater getting trounced in a landslide. (When Goldwater, the Republicans' standard-bearer, voted against the Civil Rights Act on constitutional grounds, almost overnight the Democrats found themselves with millions more black members—even though a far higher percentage of Republicans in Congress voted for both the Civil Rights Act and Voting Rights Act than did Democrats.) And, as it turned out, LBJ's words at Howard University did not translate to urgent action. Passing the landmark civil rights bills in 1964 and 1965 was hard enough; coming up with billions of dollars in the form of direct payments, modeled loosely on Germany's compensation to Holocaust survivors, would be far more difficult, and maybe impossible. Martin, though, could not be deterred.

In a speech we composed together the year before his death, he pointed out that liberating the Negro from chattel slavery in 1863 and then expecting him to compete overnight in the free market had been a symptom of depraved absurdity, because nothing ever was done to counterweigh the fact that, by law, the black man had been kept illiterate and penniless. Worse, at the very moment that freed slaves were discovering that the forty acres and a mule they'd been promised were no more real than the proverbial check in the mail, the army was clearing Indian lands and the federal government was inviting both white citizens and European immigrants to come and grab what they could. Heartbreakingly, though America had brought the black man here against his will, she now offered him no place in her manifest destiny. In short, Martin said, "freedom for the Negro was freedom without bread to eat or land to cultivate."

His arguments were sound, even inarguable, and the history irrefutable. But apparently there were not enough "fair-minded" citizens moved by them to incite politicians into action. Reparations for blacks appeared to be a distant dream, and doing little more than punishing federally funded bigots wouldn't change black America's reality soon enough. So Martin began wondering about what might happen if Negroes weren't the only beneficiaries of these proposed compensatory damages. What would happen if poor whites, too, benefited? Pushing for that, he decided, very well might initiate a rising tide of support that lifted black boats, as well.

In retrospect, I think it was a mistake that Martin began packaging a black reparations argument with what he called a "Bill of Rights for the Disadvantaged." His strategy, well-intentioned and reasonable, was to draw broad support from other national organizations, especially labor unions, as a way of appealing to the masses of voters and thereby closing the deal.

But by including the rescue of "a large stratum of the forgotten white poor," and insisting, "I do not intend that this program of economic aid should only go to the Negro; it should benefit the disadvantaged of *all* races," he inadvertently undermined the eloquent justice of reparations for black America.

Who, after all, could seriously deny that GIs were being compensated for their previous, if short, deprivations? Or that the United States had enticed millions of Europeans to these shores and presented them with the ultimate welcoming gift—land? Only racists could honestly contend that these arguments should not apply at least equally, if not more deservedly, to millions of Negroes. And yet, even most fair-minded citizens never considered the righteousness of paying damages to Negroes who had been here for centuries and suffered far more than the average soldier.

I know that Martin felt genuine despair for the plight of poor white folk, the millions who were horribly disadvantaged and "on the outskirts of hope." Their heartbreaking circumstances spoke to his deepest convictions that no human being should have to live in abject degradation, especially in the world's richest country. So it wasn't merely a political calculation that inspired him to remember those whom progress had left behind. Far from it.

And yet, the circumstances that begat whites' destitution weren't strictly comparable with the Negro's. In otherwise free societies, explanations for poverty are many; some have to do with class, some with opportunity, or with skill, talent, and ambition. In an unfree society, which was where blacks resided, there are other reasons. Whites, whatever else their circumstances, lived in a society that allowed them the liberty to take up residence in another colony, another country, another continent, and work at another trade without bounty hunters chasing them and masters hacking off their feet as punishment. Not the white but only the Negro was, by law, made the property of others and deprived of the most basic human freedoms. Not the white but only the Negro was, by law and custom, prevented and prohibited from rising to the level of his innate talents and greatest ambitions. The seventeenth, eighteenth, and nineteenth centuries were replete with whites who rose far higher than the humble circumstances of their birth. Few Negroes did the same.

All things being equal, all things were not equal between blacks and whites, even the poorest of whites. The truth is, and was, that no whites had been brought here in chains. They had not, as a race, been considered private property to be sold, traded, bartered, even murdered. They had not, without their consent, been stripped of their language, customs, and culture, nor prevented from educating themselves. Yes, other circumstances may have conspired against them, but the awesome power of the United States government was not one of them.

I don't blame Martin's "Bill of Rights for the Disadvantaged" alone, nor his developing view that poverty was perhaps more about class than race, for opening a door that allowed more people through than should have been for this *specific purpose*; his voice advocating for wider inclusion and economic "justice" for all was just the most prominent and influential of many voices—black, white, brown, yellow.

But if Martin were here today, I believe he'd look back and see that his moral arguments for reparations of some kind would have been better confined to the race of people whose four-hundred-year history in this country deserved unique consideration from at least the U.S. Treasury. It may sound crude, but in the 1960s, the hearts and minds of, say, bigoted Cadillac dealers would've been transformed a lot faster if they'd seen the grandsons of slaves coming through their doors with piles of cash in hand—and the wherewithal to buy another new car the following year, too. Oh, and maybe even a dealership themselves.

But now that the terms of the debate had changed, in late 1967 LBJ amended his executive order to cover discrimination not just on the basis of race but also on the basis of gender. Affirmative action had become a tar baby, as President Nixon confirmed a few years later (after Martin's death), when his Justice and Labor departments, and his administration's Equal Opportunity and Civil Service commissions, published a joint acknowledgment that their policies from the earliest days of Nixon's presidency had been to establish "goals and timetables" as a "proper means for helping to implement the nation's commitment to equal employment opportunity." It was, God knows, easy enough to hate Nixon for any number of reasons, but his attitude about race wouldn't have surprised anyone who remembered that, as vice president in 1959, he'd headed the President's Committee on Government Contracts that called for corrective steps for employer "indifference" to discrimination.

In 1959, such discrimination as Nixon had noted referred specifically to Negroes. Ten or eleven years later, discrimination was a big tent that included almost everyone but your average white man. And since that day, the issue of affirmative action, quotas, set-asides, and other indirect forms of reparations has been hopelessly clouded.

What would Martin say?

2

For the last decade or so it's become fashionable in some circles to contend that Martin Luther King didn't support favoritism in hiring and admissions as a way of rectifying historical inequities. Dozens of Martin's quotations, removed from their context, are cited endlessly to support the argument that all Martin desired was a level playing field. One of his most famous proclamations—"I have a dream that my four little children will one day live in a nation where they will not be judged by the color of their skin but by the content of their character"—has been turned into a rallying mantra by those who maintain that the great man himself, a secular saint, would abhor the notion of his own people receiving handouts or special consideration in hiring and admission to institutes of learning.

Well, such people are right only in the sense that Martin's first and best choice was reparations; anything less he considered the booby prize. When it appeared that only the booby prize would be possible, he insisted that government had a moral obligation, having created the Negro's harsh conditions, to initiate and fund programs that would affirmatively benefit those Americans who'd been impacted by slavery and its legacies. Nothing I ever heard him say, in hundreds of conversations, meetings, strategy sessions, or conventions, contradicted that.

But because he didn't live long enough to see these policies implemented as they are now, his allegiance to intellectual honesty would have led him to consider the totality of what affirmative action has wrought. The question is not what Martin Luther King favored forty years ago, because the record is clear. The real question is what Martin would say now, after taking inventory of where we are today. And where we are, he'd undoubtedly admit, is far from where we were on the day he was murdered. There has indeed been progress, an astonishing amount of it.

It's not difficult for me to imagine Martin waking up, like Rip Van Winkle from a long sleep, and having to rub his eyes at the colossal number of black elected officials—from dog catcher to school board head to mayor to congressman—particularly in, of all places, the South; nationally, it's been a hundredfold increase in thirty-five years. (Mississippi, for example, now boasts a higher percentage of black elected officials than any other state.)

Martin would see a robust and rising black middle class, unimaginable in his day, even if the total household net worth of the black middle class still lags behind whites' net worth—a fact owed in part to inherited wealth on the one hand and strictly first-generation wealth on the other.

He'd see whites of all ages and everywhere in the country proudly wearing the jerseys of their favorite black athletes—their heroes!—and he'd also see many of those athletes earning tens of millions of dollars not only on the field but as spokesmen for corporate America.

He'd see Hollywood producing movies and television shows that star and feature black actors in numbers that reach or exceed the percentage of African Americans in the overall population.

He'd see a woman named Oprah wield more power in the popular culture and influence over the national conversation than perhaps anyone ever, as if she owned a magic wand capable of making and breaking people, places, things, and ideas.

He'd see that blacks had risen to the executive suites, even the chairmanships, of Fortune 500 companies.

He'd see big-city police and fire departments recruiting and hiring blacks as though they were the preferred race.

He'd see black entrepreneurs patenting, marketing, and succeeding as never before.

He'd see black home ownership at historic highs, and black small businesses opening and succeeding even in predominantly white areas.

He'd see black authors reaching national readerships and sections of otherwise white bookstores devoted specifically to black themes.

He'd see a black chairman of the Joint Chiefs, a black Army Chief of Staff, and two black secretaries of state—the position fifth in succession to the presidency.

He'd sit with me at the Martin Luther King Institute at Stanford University and, over dinner, hear the president of his alma mater, Morehouse College, a black man whose black wife is a prominent physician (courtesy of Harvard Med), deliver the astonishing news that opportunities for black college graduates are manifold at traditionally black colleges; these institutions, say the president, are where major corporations go *first* to recruit their next best and brightest employees.

And he'd see a black man considered a sustained, serious contender for the presidency of the United States; a man who for a long time outpolled and outearned in political contributions any other candidate of either party; a man whose major asset and qualification, this early in his career, is, ironically, his black skin.

Being fair-minded, if that's all Martin saw, he'd declare that we'd done it, we'd won, we'd made it, hallelujah, we'd reached the top of that mountain and tasted the elixir of glorious triumph at last; that whites had opened their hearts and minds; that, in his absence, the country had become as colorblind as any society of human beings ever could be, and that young black Americans lucky enough to come of age early in the twenty-first century can participate fully in the American Dream without the manacles of racism holding them down.

And then, after applauding the programs, quotas, set-asides, and preferences that helped make at least some of this progress possible, he'd end them all—every last program—by shouting, "Thank God almighty, we're free at last."

And you know what? In a larger sense, he'd be right about all of that.

But . . .

But then, after the glittering successes had stopped blinding him, he'd see far too many young blacks acquainted with the justice system.

He'd see young blacks killed at a rate dozens of times that of young whites—killed not by whites but by each other. In tribal gangs.

He'd see 70 percent of black babies born to unwed mothers—almost three times the percentage considered scandalous when he left us in 1968—nearly all of them in homes without fathers present.

He'd see young black men investing more stock in their future as basketball players than as architects, astronauts, and attorneys—and a subculture called "gangsta" in which doing well in school deserves the ultimate diss, "acting white," while calling each other "nigga" and "ho" is perfectly acceptable.

He'd see an icon of nearly fifty years in the black community, Bill Cosby, excoriated and ostracized for speaking truth to power about the state of young black America's values and work ethic.

He'd see blacks calling blacks "Uncle Tom" and "sell-out" and "inauthentic" for belonging to the wrong political party—Republican; and Michael Steele, a man on the verge of becoming the first black senator from Maryland, suffering insults daily from blacks who apparently didn't share any pride in the history he could have made because he wasn't the "right" kind of black man; and civil rights groups staying mostly silent when cartoonists lampooned the conservatism of the first black female secretary of state, Condoleezza Rice, with caricatures of her that would've been at home in 1920s jigaboo comic strips.

Martin would see black women reaching college at unprecedented rates, though without a reasonable expectation that they will one day marry equally successful black men and raise healthy-minded, ambitious black children together.

He'd see so-called black leaders convincing young blacks that they'd been born with one foot in the grave in a world that hates them, and that they're doomed to fail if someone doesn't offer them a handout as opposed to an opportunity.

And then he'd see black males at Stanford and Harvard and Northwestern whose admissions are considered freebies, their matriculations do-goods, and their degrees inconsequential by whites and Asians who've come to believe that, thanks to different entry criteria for different races, blacks can't succeed on their own.

And finally Martin would see serious academics, who wish to investigate whether well-intended affirmative action programs are actually good for African Americans or whether they harm them through unintended consequences, shouted down and silenced—by other academics. (See: UCLA law professor Richard Sander.)

In the early twenty-first century, these two black Americas coexist. And both of them, it seems, are products or by-products of the Movement. In reconciling them—the accomplishments versus the breakdowns—Martin would have to answer how much of a role affirmative action played in the creation of the former. And whether it also contributed in any way to the latter.

Martin was a dreamer, yes, but first he was a realist. He didn't dream dreams that he didn't trust could come true. And the fact that so many of them did would have confirmed to him that the rest were possible, too. But how to make that so?

3

In Martin's lifetime, for a Negro to succeed he had to overcome the white pathologies that made affirmative action necessary in the first place. Today, for a black man to succeed he has to either overcome or avoid the pathologies too common in his own race, no matter that many of these pathologies may be considered the residue of slavery's original sin. Martin would be overwhelmed by the depravity of young brothers killing each other with guns and themselves with despair, and with the gangsta subculture that produces what African American social critic Stanley Crouch referred to as "the most dehumanizing images of black people since the dawn of minstrelsy in the nineteenth century." Even so, it's a toss-up as to whether Martin would initially be more thrilled by the substantial progress or dismayed by the viciousness.

For sake of argument, let's say that after hearing a typical Kanye West song and reading a typical rap sheet he'd try to console himself by hugging Barack Obama.

But unless Obama possesses some special magic in his hug, Martin would be inconsolable at the thought and sight of dead young men piling up in the streets and morgues like cordwood every weekend—killed not by Klansmen or free-lance racists or even the cops, but by someone who looks just like them, talks like them, acts like them. This would rip Martin's heart out, I think, because these are literally senseless killings in that they're inspired by senselessness. In war, after all, you hate the reality but you accept that the enemy, hailing from another country or ideology, intends to kill as many good guys as possible. But when the enemy is Damian from across the street, and he either covets your sneakers or doesn't like your friends, then it's not war; it's suicide, fratricide, genocide.

I don't have to wonder about Martin's reaction to this kind of killing, because I was there when real enemies killed as many good guys as they could. I was there in a Birming-ham, Alabama, church in 1963, to hear the eulogy that even he knew had no special magic to ease the grief of loved ones left behind. And I was there to see his face contorted in grief.

Those images are burned into my brain, which is appropriate to what happened on that mid-September Sunday at a time when civil rights groups had been trying to register black voters in the state's capital. And what a time it was.

Barely two weeks before, we'd exulted in the historic March on Washington, blacks and whites together, hundreds of thousands of us, a moment punctuated by Martin describing his dream. Though we never lost sight of the dangers, the atmosphere was so heady then it even seemed possible to ignore inflammatory rhetoric from Alabama governor George Wallace, who knew a thing or two about inflammatory rhetoric. At his inauguration in January, for example, he'd infamously declared: "Segregation today, segregation tomorrow, segregation forever."

And now, just a week or so after we returned from the March on Washington, he'd announced that what was necessary to stop integration were "a few first-class funerals."

Wallace's words were apparently taken as marching orders by Klansmen, one of whom got out of a blue-and-white Chevy and placed a box of some kind under the steps of the Sixteenth Street Baptist Church where young Sunday schoolers were learning their Bible lessons—lessons like love your neighbor as yourself and turn the other cheek. The man who'd placed that box, and the men who helped him, had undoubtedly gone to church, too, and surely grown up in Sunday school. But none of them had learned their lessons very well, for at 10:22 a.m. that box revealed itself to be a dynamite bomb.

The explosion and resulting fire, in addition to badly injuring two dozen young people, killed three 14-year-old girls and an 11-year-old girl. (Condoleezza Rice has said that she was on her way to the church when the bomb went off. You do not have to love, like, or even appreciate her to get a sense of how these four lost lives might have impacted the world.)

When he heard what happened, Martin had shouted in rage, calling the bombing "the most dastardly act of barbarism" he'd seen in the course of the struggle. He wondered whether he should send telegrams to church leaders and President Kennedy, asking for a national day of mourning. I and others thought that was a good idea, and the request was sent. But the president, who would himself have only two months to live, did not declare it. So it was left to Martin to speak for the national conscience.

In his eulogy, Martin contended that Addie Mae Collins, Carole Robertson, Cynthia Wesley, and Denise McNair were now "the martyred heroines of a holy crusade for freedom and human dignity." Their deaths, he said, had sent pointed messages to clergy who'd remained silent or scared; to politicians selling "the stale bread of hatred and the spoiled meat of racism"; and to the Negro who "passively accepts the evil system of segregation, and stands on the sidelines in the midst of a mighty struggle for justice."

But this holy crusade he spoke of does not, and cannot, apply to our inner-city murders; there's nothing noble or righteous about them, and the dead are not martyrs to a cause. Neither do Martin's final words that day speak to those who fall dead on a typical Saturday night in the 'hood, or to their families, or to our society that permits such wanton slaughter:

"Your children did not live long, but they lived well. . . . Where they died and what they were doing when death came will remain a marvelous tribute to each of you and an eternal epitaph to each of them. They died not in a den or dive, nor were they hearing and telling filthy jokes at the time of their death. . . .

"Goodnight sweet princesses. May the flight of angels take thee to thy eternal rest."

Martin did not make it through those final lines without breaking down. It was the first time I'd seen him cry in public.

Were he to be here with us today, eulogizing any of the dozens of inner-city youth killed by other inner-city youth, I don't believe that his tears would be wet with grief. Instead, they'd be tears of anger at killings more pointless than those caused by any war in history. You see, even in Birmingham, at a time when the police and government did nothing to protect Negroes and the governor actually incited violence, the Sixteenth Street Baptist Church reopened a year later with an inaugural sermon preached by Rev. H. O. Hester—a white man. So indeed, those four young girls had not, as Martin declared, died in vain. And they were, as he called them, "martyred heroines of a holy crusade" for redemption.

But what redemption can be found for a community destroying itself in an orgy of violence whose proximate cause is alleged disrespect? The tribalism of it is a fact too terrible to bear.

Which is why, for obvious reasons, Martin would immediately begin looking for solutions the way he always did: by working backward to find the source of the problem so that it could be corrected. And in 2008, the inescapable problem, the one he'd consider the sick trunk of the tree with contagious limbs, would be the deterioration of the black family.

The term itself, "black family," has become almost an oxymoron these days when so many homes are headed by single moms whose former sexual partner—the inseminator—wouldn't recognize his own offspring in a lineup. Genius is hardly required to grasp the statistic that the vast majority of men on death row, black and white, grew up without fathers, as did the vast majority of teenage girls who *choose* to have babies while still babies themselves. Nor is an advanced economics degree necessary to explain why intact black families—mother and father together under the same roof—almost never fall below the poverty line, even if they've each earned no more than high school degrees.

Having seen Martin devour volume after volume of history as he searched for explanations back when, I can imagine him powering through forty years of books, newspapers, magazines, movies, video, and recordings to see where things went bad.

And I believe I know what he'd conclude. He'd blame, without apology, the inadvertent social and economic consequences of the welfare-on-demand state for worsening much of what it was intended to mitigate.

In 1970 the Supreme Court ruled (*Goldberg v. Kelly*) that welfare payments and other government subsidies were a form of "new property" and therefore a legal entitlement, thus giving blacks equal access to programs like Aid to Families with Dependent Children. At the time, this was considered a victory for civil rights. And it was until it wasn't.

By then, AFDC was decades old and had been applied in various ways over the years, usually to favor widows. But during the heady blush of LBJ's Great Society, rules and guidelines were relaxed considerably, to the point where welfare advocates were able to more or less abolish the sometimes onerous work requirement for mothers that, they argued, caused mothers to choose between caring for their children or starving. Their reasoning was persuasive but shortsighted. Alas, since the work requirement still applied to fathers present in the house—and the program set no limit on the number of additional children for which a single mother could receive additional payments—the net effect was to make AFDC and other assistance programs a viable career choice for single mothers who were living in a society that limited their outside choices anyway. It turned young black women into baby machines and young black men into conscienceless inseminators.

These consequences hurt the whole country. White Americans, too, sought reward for behavior that had always been considered taboo. But because of their smaller numbers in the population, already higher rates of illegitimacy (as Assistant Secretary of Labor Daniel Patrick Moynihan infamously warned against in 1965), preexisting financial disadvantage, and institutionalized barriers to opportunity built by racism, blacks were disproportionately drawn to and hurt by welfare as it had evolved. And in that they were aided and abetted by otherwise well-meaning people, legislators and advocates alike, who kept arguing that no one *wants* to be on welfare or wants to *stay* on welfare. (Of course, a great many intellectuals also believed that the Soviet Union was a workers' paradise.) And if they *were* on welfare, went the argument, well, there had to be a damn good reason: "Maybe that's all they're capable of."

To my mind, as there would be to Martin's, there was a tincture of polite racism in all those good intentions and pity—the implicit notion that the very Negro who had survived centuries of cruel servitude and then increased his numbers during a hundred years of, at best, merciless indifference, could not possibly be expected to do whatever it took to succeed. How come no one ever made that argument during the Middle Passage or cotton harvest?

I assure you, none of us working for civil rights *at that time*—not Martin, not Stanley Levison, not the SCLC or the NAACP, and certainly not Malcolm X—intended for whites or the white power structure to feel *pity* for Negroes.

Pity is a destructive force in that it seduces the one being pitied into believing that he's pitiable, leading him eventually to pity himself. That's how he becomes dehumanized and emasculated, his diligence undermined. And as Martin knew, the last thing, literally the *very* last thing, black America needed was an incentive not to excel.

"We've got to get segregation off their backs," he told me. "It provides a ready-made excuse for why they can't succeed."

This belief was in fact why, in late 1961, Martin asked President Kennedy personally to issue a "second Emancipation Proclamation" that would outlaw "all segregation," and make every form of it unconstitutional. (One of my unofficial duties was to meet with Malcolm X and report back to Martin, who for political reasons couldn't meet with him, on what was said. Malcolm didn't care a whit about integration; quite the opposite. But neither did he want to show up Martin in their common goal of eliminating white racism. He once joked to me, "You tell Martin to tell the white man that if he don't listen and deal with him, the white man's gonna have to deal with Malcolm X." At least I think it was a joke.)

Nothing mattered more to Martin than the pursuit of excellence—his own and others. He contended that the only way the masses of blacks in America would indeed be judged by the content of their character and not the color of their skin was through the pursuit of excellence; and he believed that if Negroes could get it in their minds that there was success in the simple pursuit of excellence—regardless of outcome, regardless of obstacles—that the Movement would mostly win itself. He said, "A man should do his job so well that the living, the dead, and the unborn could do it no better." He said, "If it falls to your lot to be a street sweeper, sweep streets like Michelangelo painted pictures, like Shakespeare wrote poetry, like Beethoven composed music; sweep streets so well that all the hosts of heaven and earth will have to pause and say, 'Here lived a great street sweeper, who swept his job well.'"

What worried Martin was that the residue of segregation might act as an insidious toxin in those who'd suffered under it, a warning suggested by the Old Testament, with which he was intimately familiar. After the Hebrews escape their bondage in Egypt, God forces them to wander forty years in the desert, until the last former slave is dead, because he wants everyone who enters the promised land to be truly free, untainted by the bitter memory of servitude. To Martin, the analogy was that if Negroes too constrained by the past could not even *pretend* that they were free and were glad to be free—and willing to use their freedom in the pursuit of excellence—then they would never truly *be* free.

Alas, Martin's fear seems to have come true in modern black America. Too many of us have been wandering aimlessly in a sort of desert these forty years since his death—I'll resist the temptation to call him "black Moses"—though the promised land is there for the entering.

What would Martin say? He'd say that the cost of admission today isn't an affirmative action job or slot in school. It's the pursuit of excellence.

4

Like me, Martin was a fan of the German philosopher Hegel, whose unifying theory of history held that any strong movement (the thesis) begets a like reaction (the antithesis), thus creating a collision between the two that results in a third entity (the synthesis), which in turn becomes the new status quo (the thesis). This appears to be how history has moved through the ages, and Martin would be the first to see how the dynamic applies to affirmative action programs circa 2008.

He would, I believe, acknowledge that the conditions that produced the need for affirmative action in the first place are probably irrelevant now that qualified, ambitious blacks are desired by both employers and universities. This doesn't, of course, necessarily mean blacks don't still need more help than they're getting. A simple look at the statistics regarding black academic achievement is a compelling slap in the face. But at this point, Martin would first ask why such a gap exists. And then he'd suggest that the cost of continuing affirmative action programs may no longer be worth the benefit.

It's clear, or should be, to anyone but the most entrenched race pimp that the majority of whites either wish blacks well or don't give a damn one way or another; and that at a certain point—a point we may have already reached—their good-will, à la Hegel, begins to dissipate because of what they see, rightly or wrongly, as handouts from a society that doesn't institutionally impede black progress as it once did. From the majority white perspective, blacks are entirely capable of succeeding on their own—an attitude, ironically, that sometimes puts them at odds with modern "black leaders."

Sure, there are still bigots out there. But thanks to authentic progress and a culture that no longer sanctions open racism, they're not as obvious about their prejudices, which has the effect of making them less powerful than they once were, since they can rarely be certain that their colleagues are as bigoted as they are without blowing their cover. Now, supervisors at least have to smile and shake the young black man's hand and pretend to interview him earnestly before tossing his application into the wastebasket.

That such morons exist is a fact of life. They may be 10 percent of the population—or more. Better, let's say they're 20 percent. Even 25. But that, as Martin would agree, is actually the good news: bigots are now a minority. And it's a fatal trap to hold off trying to succeed in the belief that there will ever come a time, or a society, without haters. All things considered, this may be the least prejudiced country in history. Today, the only thing in the way of a black man's aspirations is himself. If he gives up at the first closed door or shows up at that interview wearing gangsta clothes, he's either not serious about success or unprepared for the real world.

One can reasonably argue that young black adults for whom doors have always opened based on the color of their skin are unprepared for the world most of us live in. In the real world, what they learned at the University of Michigan, or wherever their skin color granted them easier access, is, maybe for the first time, more important to their accomplishments than the color of their skin, because an employer is essentially renting that knowledge in the hopes of making himself or his company more successful. There are no freebies here in the real world; jobs are strictly a business proposition. Which is why special considerations received in the past by that young black may cause him or her to expect that doors will always be open, that dress and speech are irrelevant, and that performance is secondary. Affirmative action today is akin to the aphorism about leading horses to water: just as they still have to drink, the recipients of affirmative action still have to think.

The world we live in now, Martin would see, isn't inherently unfriendly to the thoughts of a young black. So what we risk by continuing to insist on programs that discriminate against one racial group for the benefit of another, he'd

point out, is a loss of white amity. True, the most militant blacks who read this are likely to say, "Screw the white
man," just as they did when Martin insisted on nonviolent
protests. But ignoring the white man is as self-defeating as
showing up for a job interview at IBM wearing duds from
the 50 Cent collection.

This is, for at least the foreseeable future, a world in
which whites generally make the big decisions. And at
long last—regardless of whether they have good souls
or are bowing to the gods of political correctness—they
no longer hire or admit only those who look like them. I
doubt that in his heart of hearts, Martin could have fore-
seen a time, forty years on, when the color of a prospec-
tive corporate employee would be nearly irrelevant to the
issue of whether the applicant can excel. This is extraordinary progress. But at some point a plurality of whites
are likely to ask what's the use of coming so far, so fast,
so well, in terms of losing (or hiding) their prejudice, if
black people don't acknowledge, let alone appreciate, the
progress they've made.

It's a good rule of thumb, in child-rearing as well as in
politics, to praise the kind of behavior you want more of.

I remember thinking frequently about Martin during
the harsh debate in 1996, before President Clinton signed
a bill ending "welfare as we know it." Advocates for the bill
said that it would be good for America—and even better
for those who'd come to think of welfare as their jobs; having to earn their way in the world instead of relying on a
government handout, they'd soon discover self-respect and
earn their way into the middle class, if not higher.

Critics, on the other hand, predicted that the sudden
cessation of welfare benefits would throw millions into the
street, where they'd die starving in the gutters. In fact,

when Hillary Clinton publicly supported her husband's signing the bill that Congress had sent him, she lost one of her closest friends and longtime advisers, Marian Wright Edelman, the (black) chairman of the Children's Defense Fund, who announced that she was certain that the bill, if enacted, would leave a "moral blot on his presidency and on our nation." Her husband, Peter Edelman, protested the president's signing of the bill by resigning his post as assistant secretary of health and human services, then wrote an article titled "The Worst Thing Bill Clinton Has Done" that predicted nothing less than a social holocaust of crime, malnutrition, infant mortality, and alcohol and drug abuse.

In truth, the bill was one of the highlights of the Bill Clinton presidency, and if historians improbably decide that that's all there was to the Clinton legacy, the man should feel no shame.

Martin Luther King would have been neither disappointed nor angry with the welfare reform bill. On the contrary, he would have seen it as an opportunity—believing, I think, that it has benefited black Americans disproportionately by removing a major incentive not to excel.

By the same calculation, and against the same sort of angry rhetoric and doomsday forecasts, he would insist on an immediate end to affirmative action as we know it.

But . . .

But there'd be a but.

5

And the but is a simple tradeoff. Martin would trade affirmative action heads-up for the one thing that can, in today's world, make quotas, set-asides, and special preferences utterly obsolete and also redundantly irrelevant: quality education for all young people. That means, particularly, a Manhattan Project type of commitment for rebuilding and restaffing urban schools.

No one can seriously argue that inner-city schools across the United States—where black students are more likely than white students to attend—are in most ways better than the old one-room schoolhouses of Jim Crow Mississippi. At least in those schools, despite their lack of facilities, students were expected to learn. And learn they did. Or, if nothing else, they had to pay attention and practice self-discipline; sassing a teacher meant being unable to sit down for a week.

The situation in modern urban schools is a national tragedy deserving of national scorn—with plenty of blame to go around: from parents who, if they're even around, rarely insist in any meaningful or concerted way that administrators and teachers do their jobs, to the teachers' unions, which have manifestly valued their members' perks and salaries above the good of the students.

Thanks to the powerful National Education Association, it's just barely easier to fire a useless teacher than it is to execute a mass murderer in Vermont (where there's no death penalty). And because of the way public schools are funded, based on attendance, teachers are encouraged to move kids along from grade to grade, regardless of whether they've mastered the previous year's coursework; the fear is that kids held back because they can't count to 4 will feel discouraged enough to drop out if they have to repeat the tenth grade.

In black households, where barely three out of ten children are growing up with both a mom and a dad at home, television has become a de facto nanny. Fifty percent of black fourth graders spend at least five hours a day in front of the tube—and that's on school days; weekends are worse—compared to only 20 percent of white fourth graders.

According to the National Center for Education Statistics, black students are already behind by the time they start kindergarten, meaning that they possess significantly less general knowledge and, as two follows one, exhibit lesser capacity for reading and math. From there the mess only gets deeper.

Fewer than half of black students who make it as far as the ninth grade later graduate with a high school diploma. In places like Los Angeles, where illegal immigration has utterly changed the complexion—and operative language—of inner-city schools, the atmosphere often has more in common with a maximum-security prison than it does with a serious institution of learning. It's a sad irony that this ends up preparing too many children for the kind of place where they'll be spending much of their adult lives.

Meanwhile, the College Board—the group that administers the Scholastic Aptitude Tests, which help determine applicants' eligibility for college admission—has reported that "as a group, black students in the twelfth grade actually score lower on reading tests than eighth-grade whites. The same is true in math, history, and geography. Overall, more than 40 percent of black high school seniors tested below the basic skill in reading."

This means that at a school which grades on a curve—most if not all schools—an A student in the eleventh grade may not be able to multiply two 3-digit numbers without the aid of a calculator, or comprehend, say, *The Catcher in the Rye*. Imagine what an employer thinks when that A student she's hired turns out to be innumerate and nearly illiterate. Then imagine what happens to another A student whose grades and skin color got him into a more prestigious university than his scholastic achievements deserved. How the hell can he compete against other kids whose education has been far superior to his? Even a second-rate education is better than what he got. No wonder students admitted under more generous affirmative action guidelines take longer to graduate than other students, if they even stick with it that long, given their enormously high dropout rates caused by frustration and feelings of inadequacy.

The consequences of a failed education are lifelong misery, both for the individual and for society. Martin would agree that our country wouldn't have to import as many engineers, mathematicians, and programmers from Asia and elsewhere if our inner-city schools were turning out students capable of advanced thinking—if, going on five decades after the Civil Rights Act, African American students, on average, weren't the country's weakest at all ages, in all subjects.

Instead of producing proud black scholars, we're turning out generation after generation of young people whose prospects are so diminished that life is more hopeless than hopeful, and the concept of "future" is answered by where they'll be hanging out tomorrow; the day after that is already too far ahead. With little to live for and dreams that can't be dreamed because they seem like they're impossible anyway, it's not a mystery why 13 percent of the U.S. population—that is, our 30 million African Americans—account for more than half of all murders and robberies. That's bad enough, but wait. If you consider that almost all the perps are men, you're talking about less than 7 percent of the population committing that mayhem. Then reflect on the fact that violent crimes are the near-exclusive domain of

young men, and you have to swallow hard before acknowl-
edging that perhaps 4 percent of America's population is
robbing and murdering at a rate more than a dozen times
its proportion to that population.

The punch line to this sick joke is that these murderers
and robbers who've been "keeping it real" and not "acting white" are mostly murdering and robbing other blacks,
many of them as innocent and full of promise as those four
girls from Birmingham.

It's true that better schools and teachers, by themselves,
wouldn't make these problems vanish overnight. But it's
the place Martin Luther King, I'm sure, would choose to
start for the simple reason that a child who finds refuge
and stimulation in a school for seven hours a day—more,
likely, than the amount he's at home—can be inspired to
pursue excellence himself, despite whatever obstacles his
parents, friends, and neighborhood might lay in his path.
Then that one child's example can motivate another, and
another, until one day "acting black" means doing well—
as well as a group of bright young Negroes did a century
ago, when debaters at black colleges regularly outpointed
white students from America's best universities.

Affirmative action, Martin would say, has been a boost,
and benefited any number of people, but its time and use-
fulness have come and gone. So long as what replaces it is
the level playing field of equal opportunity that only a quality education can provide, there won't be anything wrong
with black America that black Americans won't quickly fix.

Pursue excellence and the rest will take care of itself.
That's what Martin would say.

FOUR

WHAT WOULD MARTIN SAY ABOUT ILLEGAL IMMIGRATION?

BY ANY MEASURE, 1965 WAS A HISTORIC YEAR IN American history, at least as regards civil rights. Thanks in large part to the televised demonstrations in Selma and Montgomery that had riveted the country's attention and stirred its outrage, the two houses of Congress overwhelmingly passed the Voting Rights Act of 1965, which had been sent to them by President Johnson ten days after the first marchers were abused and beaten by police in March. Either oblivious of the symbolism or trying to make some larger point, LBJ signed the bill into law on August 6, the twentieth anniversary of the Hiroshima atomic bomb blast that was now being commemorated in demonstrations around the world.

It seems no coincidence that almost exactly one month later the mostly Filipino members of the Agricultural Workers Organizing Committee protested their wages, which were far below the federal minimum of $1.25 an hour, by walking off their job of picking table grapes in and around Delano, California. But what became known as the Delano Grape Strike gained little attention or traction until the strikers were joined by the mostly Chicano workers who belonged to the National Farm Workers Association, led by César Chávez, who was soon to be a household name. Chávez, along with his colleague Delores Huerta, was determined to merge the groups into a bona fide union, essentially modifying the National Labor Relations Act of 1935 that had granted most American workers the right to join unions but excluded certain groups, including farmworkers.

Until 1964, the possibility of such an optimistic outcome would have been all but inconceivable, given that the Mexican guest worker program begun during World War II to make up for the labor shortage was still in effect, having been extended repeatedly. But after December 31, 1964, the *braceros* (as the guest workers were known) were technically not allowed into the country, and so couldn't be used as scabs to break any more work actions or strikes. Of course, technically is not the same as actually. With more than two thousand farmworkers on strike in Delano, the strike might not have lasted more than a few weeks if the grapes had begun to wither on the vine; instead the grapes were picked by others and the strike was destined to go on and on. Like the civil rights movement from which it derived its inspiration and tactics, the strike by the aptly renamed United Farm Workers of America would eventually succeed by appealing to the conscience of ordinary Americans—those who, with their votes, tell the politicians what to do; and those who tell the store owners, with their dollars, what they will buy and what they will leave to rot on the shelves.

César Chávez was two years older than Martin Luther King. He'd been born in Arizona to a family whose cruel poverty had been caused in large part by men conning and cheating his father out of the family home. With no other choice than to become migrant workers, the Chávez family made so many moves following the crops that César attended more than thirty schools before finally giving up his studies completely in the eighth grade to pick full-time. He was later arrested for sitting in the white section of a neighborhood movie theater, and did two years of navy service right after World War II—a third-generation American without prospects for the future brighter than a life spent stooped over for pennies an hour.

"It's ironic," Chávez said, "that those who till the soil, cultivate and harvest the fruits, vegetables and other foods that fill your tables with abundance have nothing left for themselves." You don't even have to close your eyes to imagine Martin Luther King saying the same thing in a different context.

Chávez's activism began in the early 1950s, when he became a community organizer for a Chicano rights group in San Jose, California, where he'd been living in a barrio nicknamed *Sal si puedes*—"Get out if you can." Though he lacked Martin's formal schooling and rigorous academic background, he, too, found himself as the right man in the right place at the right time for the right cause. Leading voter registration drives and righting endemic discrimination against Mexicans in the 1950s, he rose to become director of the Community Service Organization, then used that experience as a stepping-stone to form the National Farm Workers Association. His inspiration, he said frequently, came from Martin Luther King and the burgeoning civil rights movement. This was fitting, because in most ways, he and Martin were fighting the same fight in different theaters of operation. It was a fight against poverty—not just financial poverty, but also poverty of the soul, a condition created by hopelessness. The hope that Martin gave black people, César Chávez gave brown people.

"We seek our basic God-given rights as human beings," Chávez said, words that might just as well have come from Martin Luther King. As were these: "Nonviolence is not inaction. It is not discussion. It is not for the timid or weak. . . . Nonviolence is hard work. It is the willingness to sacrifice. It is the patience to win."

And these: "If you give yourself totally to the nonviolent struggle for peace and justice, you also find that people give you their hearts and you will never go hungry and never be alone."

A year after Martin led the Selma-to-Montgomery march, Chávez led strikers and supporters on a three-hundred-mile march from the agricultural fields of California's San Joaquin Valley to the state's capital, Sacramento, where ten thousand supporters helped them get at least one major grower to recognize the union.

Chávez frequently fasted for long periods to call attention to his cause. He organized boycotts, was jailed and beaten, and never raised his fists to retaliate, only his voice. The union's idea to invite consumers in America and around the world to boycott all California table grapes as a way of forcing the growers to capitulate eventually succeeded, with about 15 million Americans consciously choosing not to buy California grapes after they heard endorsements of the strike from the likes of Martin, Robert Kennedy, Hubert Humphrey, and Eugene McCarthy. (Richard Nixon, on the other hand, joked that he'd gladly eat double helpings.) What the Civil Rights Act of 1964 and Voting Rights Act of 1965 were to the country's disenfranchised, the settling of the Delano strike and recognition of the United Farm

Workers by the AFL-CIO were to the tens of thousands of Americans who pick the food we eat. Wages rose and benefits like health insurance were offered. By any measure, it was a great victory, even if only a first step.

"As brothers in the fight for equality, I extend the hand of fellowship and goodwill and wish continuing success to you and your members," Martin telegraphed Chávez in Delano. "The fight for equality must be fought on many fronts—in the urban slums, in the sweatshops of the factories and fields. Our separate struggles are really one—a struggle for freedom, for dignity, and for humanity. You and your valiant fellow workers have demonstrated your commitment to righting grievous wrongs forced upon exploited people. We are together with you in spirit and in determination that our dreams for a better tomorrow will be realized."

Clearly, César Chávez and Martin Luther King were brothers in spirit, and it is right that both should be honored with holidays, streets, parks, libraries, and schools bearing their names.

They also shared something else: the belief that government must be compelled to act in the best interests of its people but that people too often accept government policy as a kind of moral dictum. An example that Chávez cited frequently, and Martin would agree with, is the wink-wink-nudge-nudge open border that allows countless numbers of illegal immigrants to flood across and either take or undermine jobs done by Americans, especially brown and black Americans.

2

The Voting Rights Act of 1965 allowed monumental numbers of Negroes to register and mark their X's on the ballot, leading in the four-plus decades since to countless thousands of blacks holding elected office. For farmworkers, though, César Chávez's victory has been diminished by the fact that their real wages have held steady, if not fallen, over the years. In fact, when Chávez died at age 67, in 1993, he had lived long enough to see his beloved union fall into virtual obsolescence, a victim of an illegal-worker deluge beginning in the 1980s.

At a rally celebrating the fifth federally observed Martin Luther King Jr. Day in 1990, Chávez spoke to the crowd about his role model and colleague: "During my first fast in 1968," he said, "Dr. King reminded me that our struggle was his struggle, too. He sent me a telegram which said, 'Our separate struggles are really one. A struggle for freedom, for dignity, and for humanity.' I was profoundly moved that someone facing such a tremendous struggle himself would take the time to worry about a struggle taking place on the other side of the continent. Just as Dr. King was a disciple of Gandhi and Christ, we must now be Dr. King's disciples. . . . Just as Bull Connor turned the dogs loose on nonviolent marchers in Alabama, the growers turn armed foremen on innocent farmworkers in California. . . . My friends, if we are going to end the suffering, we must use the same people power that vanquished injustice in Montgomery, Selma, and Birmingham. . . . In our life-and-death struggle for justice, we have turned to the court of last resort, the American people. And the people are ruling in our favor. . . . If we fail to learn that each and every person can make a difference, then we will have betrayed Dr. King's life's work."

The two men were brothers in nonviolent arms, and it's doubtful that they would've disagreed on anything more philosophically substantive than who to root for at a football game. But not being here to speak for himself now, César Chávez seems to have been coopted by the *reconquista* movement—the notion that the Southwest once belonged to and should again belong to Mexico; it aims to accomplish, in de facto fashion, through sheer numbers on the ground, what could not be accomplished politically, or achieved on the battlefield in the Mexican War (1846–48), when the United States annexed parts of Arizona, Colorado, New Mexico, and Wyoming and all of California, Nevada, and Utah.

Ironically, that kind of radical goal espoused by La Raza, MEChA, and other *reconquista* advocacy groups conforms to the aims of Big Business, which worships at the Bank of Cheap Labor, and of government, which usually bows to the whims of Big Business—so the anticapitalist radicals and major corporations are fighting for the same thing. At the same time, this population redistribution may benefit Mexico most of all, enriching it with $20 billion *a year* sent home by illegals who have in essence been exiled to the United States by a government that cannot develop its own economy enough to create jobs capable of offering subsistence pay for even its hardest workers. Of course, Mexico has barely educated those same people, so the ones who come here are too often illiterate, at least functionally so. The kind of work for which they qualify hardly exists in Mexico but abounds in this country.

In his final years Chávez had no choice but to embrace, with one arm, the concept of illegal immigration, if only as a way to bolster the union whose membership had been undone by—yes—illegals. But his actions and words over the prior decades were too pointed and precise to outweigh any later expedience. In 1969, for example, he had protested the government's blind eye to illegal immigration by leading a march that attracted the support of, among others, Rev. Ralph Abernathy, Martin's old, dear friend and successor as head of the SCLC, and Walter Mondale, the Minnesota senator who would become both vice president and Democratic nominee for president.

Ten years after that, Chávez testified before a congressional subcommittee on labor and human resources, his tone anguished, frustrated, and angry at the government that was failing to enforce its own laws intended to protect its own citizens:

"For so many years," he said, "we have been involved in agricultural strikes; organizing almost thirty years as a worker, as an organizer, and as president of the union—and for all these almost thirty years it is apparent that when the farmworkers strike and their strike is successful, the employers go to Mexico and have unlimited, unrestricted use of illegal alien strikebreakers to break the strike. And, for over thirty years, the Immigration and Naturalization Service has looked the other way and assisted in the strikebreaking. I do not remember one single instance in thirty years where the immigration service has removed strikebreakers."

César Chávez was not formally educated in economics. But then, he didn't have to be; he lived daily with the real-world effects of supply and demand, seeing firsthand what happens to the value of something when the supply far exceeds its demand. If there's an endless supply of labor willing to do whatever the job happens to be—from cleaning toilets, to digging ditches, to picking grapes—an employer who doesn't fear legal consequences has no reason other than his own conscience not to hire whoever does the job minimally well at the cheapest price. No wonder, for example, fees earned by gardeners in southern California, where you almost have to speak Spanish in order to hire a gardener, have been unchanged for a decade. Gardeners know that if they ask for a raise, they can be replaced in minutes by someone willing to do the job for the same amount or maybe less.

Of course, Chávez was sympathetic to the illegals, as anyone with a heart would be. With few prospects back home, those who come here to work have no other alternative if they want to care for their families. If I were in their place, I'd sneak across the border too and do whatever I could to make a living, as would, I can assure you, Martin Luther King. (And you, too, I suspect.) So the issue has nothing to do with racism; it's strictly economics and politics. At some point, the lifeboat analogy comes into play: room for everyone means death for all.

Which is why Martin would be outraged by the greater immorality of importing a slave class into this country, especially one that has robbed so many African Americans of their hard-won livelihoods—in the building trades, for instance, and even in garbage pickup, which was after all the issue that had brought Martin to Memphis on that terrible day in 1968: like the Delano strikers, Memphis's striking sanitation workers were fighting for the city to recognize their union. Leave aside the question of why so many blacks, generations on, still find themselves qualified only for jobs traditionally considered by others as undesirable. The question is, how many blacks who held those jobs that paid wages and benefits enough to raise their families comfortably no longer work those jobs—replaced by one of the 12 to 20 million or more who have no legal status in this country and are therefore willing to be exploited?

What's happened to blacks on the low rungs of the economic ladder mirrors what happened to Chávez's farmworkers who lost their union, their clout, and their jobs to the onslaught of illegal immigrants willing to work for not much more than a thank-you. Jobs like roofing and drywall, which used to be taken disproportionately by blacks and offer middle-class wages, often with union benefits, have more and more become the domain of poorly paid illegals, many of whom are picked up in front of a Home Depot each morning. That one hears little about this displacement, except from black callers who phone largely right-wing radio talk shows to complain whenever the topic is illegal immigration, indicates that black leaders, including the Congressional Black Caucus, have calculated that their political fortunes will be enhanced more in the long run by allying themselves with millions whom they believe will one day be legalized and granted voting rights—an irony in and of itself.

Martin, I assure you, would not be so quiet. He would insist in unambiguous language, over and over, until the message had been heard, that blacks had worked too hard and too long to achieve the kind of economic opportunities that go along with racial justice. To let those gains shrivel up, he'd say, insults the memory of those who gave their all.

3

In 1997, a 22-year-old woman named Elvira Arellano from the Mexican state of Michoacan sneaked across the U.S.-Mexican border and was quickly captured by immigration agents and deported back to Mexico. Undeterred, she tried again a few days later and made it to Oregon, where she lived for three years and gave birth to a son. The son, Saul, was born a citizen of the United States, thanks to some clumsy wording in the Constitution's Fourteenth Amendment that was written and passed for the purpose of providing Negroes with further protections inadvertently not covered by the Thirteenth Amendment banning slavery. One of those protections was American citizenship. "All persons born or naturalized in the United States, and subject to the jurisdiction thereof, are citizens of the United States and of the State wherein they reside. No State shall make or enforce any law which shall abridge the privileges or immunities of citizens of the United States; nor shall any State deprive any person of life, liberty, or property, without due process of law; nor deny to any person within its jurisdiction the equal protection of the laws."

It's not really arguable, considering the history and debate of this amendment's passage immediately after the Thirteenth and just before the Fifteenth (which granted voting rights to citizens of every color), that its intention was to keep former slaves and their offspring from being deported to, say, Africa after emancipation. It had nothing to do with, say, Canadian women nine months pregnant visiting Detroit to produce American citizens. And yet, the amendment's wording has since been interpreted to mean that every child born on American soil is an American citizen and entitled to all rights and privileges pertaining thereto, including but not limited to welfare benefits. Not for nothing have countless expectant women made their way across the Mexican border and given birth to American citizens. Having an American child is seen as a type of insurance policy, if not an investment. The fact that Elvira Arellano apparently spent no appreciable time with the man who fathered her son, nor, apparently, does the boy know the man—who was not named on the birth certificate— raises the reasonable inference that she may have chosen motherhood more as an instrument of immigration policy than as an expression of maternal instinct.

With her new son, Elvira moved east to Chicago and found work cleaning floors and bathrooms at one of the world's busiest airports, O'Hare. In a sense, her unluckiest day was September 11, 2001, when the terror attacks on the United States finally, but only briefly, caused the feds to double-check the status of every airport employee. Poor Elvira was found to be using a stolen Social Security number and, on conviction, sentenced to three years probation and deportation.

But nothing is that simple in the world of illegal immigration, even when a stolen Social Security number is involved. Claiming that her son suffered from attention-deficit disorder and other maladies, Elvira enlisted the aid of church leaders, immigration rights advocates, and politicians like Illinois's Democratic senator Dick Durbin and Democratic representative Luis Gutierrez. As a result of all the noise, the Department of Homeland Security decided, in essence, to misplace her file, and Elvira was allowed to remain in this country, though without a visa or a green card.

What did she do now with her good luck? Go back to work? Raise her child quietly and plan for his future? No. She founded an illegal-alien activist group called United Latino Family and publicly advocated for making every illegal alien extant a legal alien, which would of course invite many more illegals to this side of the border. She even found herself consulting with Mexico's then-president Vicente Fox, from whose country she had fled and obviously wanted to avoid returning to. Fox was in no way offended, though; the feeling, it seems fair to say, was mutual, because he supported and encouraged her efforts to speed the exodus from Mexico and flout the laws of the United States. (The wildest imagination, I think, would be left inadequate to conjure an image of any U.S. president working on behalf of someone who fled the United States and wants to stay *illegally* in, say, France.)

Three years on, in August of 2006, the Department of Homeland Security at last sent Elvira a letter ordering her to appear at a downtown office to begin deportation. Her son, of course, was not subject to the order.

Elvira refused to appear as ordered. She and 7-year-old Saul took sanctuary in a Methodist church, all but daring the authorities to come and get her, and calling her plight and the plight of others like her "a civil rights issue." Though they were not legally constrained by the church premises and cries of "Sanctuary!" that recalled Quasimodo's rescue of the gypsy girl Esmeralda in *The Hunchback of Notre Dame*, the immigration authorities nonetheless did nothing for as long as Elvira stayed in the church.

After a year inside, perhaps feeling safe, Elvira and Saul left the church and flew to Los Angeles, where she spoke to three church congregations about the need to legalize illegal immigrants. Before she could reach the fourth church on her schedule, immigration officials arrested her and she was quickly dropped at the Mexican border subject to her original 1997 deportation order.

Hours later she stood in Tijuana facing a phalanx of cameras and microphones. "I cannot sit by now and watch the lives of mothers and fathers like me and children like Saulito be destroyed. I believe in my heart that the people of this nation do not in their hearts want to destroy our lives, our families, and our communities."

Of course, Elvira could have chosen not to break up her family and take her son with her to Mexico; instead, she left him behind with church officials, probably as a bargaining chip for her return. Days later she managed a meeting with

Mexico's new president, Felipe Calderón, who declared that deporting illegal immigrants violated principles of human rights. More to the point, he said, "Mexico does not stop at its border, that wherever there is a Mexican, there is Mexico." No mention was made of Mexico's militarization of its southern border in order to keep out Guatemalans or any other non-Mexican national who might have made the trek that far north. Nor did the Mexican president note that non-Mexicans, even those legally in the country, who deign to join Mexico's political conversation—say, by taking part in demonstrations or through public advocacy—are summarily arrested and, if lucky, deported.

But it's not President Calderón's hypocrisy regarding Mexico's immigration laws that's pertinent here. It's the idea that the president of any country felt free to mock, without consequences, another country's sovereignty. Nothing he could have said better reflects the inexorable wave heading our way and the dishonesty of our national debate on illegal immigration. What made it so significant is that no national leader, including our president, even bothered to criticize the inappropriate remark as what it was: an assault on American independence. Maybe they were too busy pandering.

4

The saga of Elvira Arellano encapsulates why Martin Luther King's attitude toward illegal immigration would not be what its supporters might hope—and indeed, what they've falsely credited him with. Martin, it should be obvious, was no anarchist, and he certainly feared making hyper-capitalism the engine of public policy.

The first thing he'd say is that, on this issue, the modifier of immigration is "illegal," and whether one substitutes the euphemism "undocumented workers" doesn't change the fact that Elvira, like everyone else who sneaks into the country or overstays a visa, is breaking a federal law.

Yes, he'd say, there are laws and then there are laws. In 1857, the Supreme Court upheld the law that said Dred Scott, a former slave living in a free state, would remain the property of his master no matter the circumstances where he resided; in sum, he was not a U.S. citizen capable of exercising civil rights. Four decades later, in *Plessy v. Ferguson*, the Court upheld the law that separated public facilities for white and colored. And it wasn't until the 1960s that the Court overturned laws prohibiting miscegenation. Obviously, not all laws are moral, and sometimes breaking the law is an act of morality.

This was the core of Martin's strategy for the civil rights movement, dividing laws into those he considered just and unjust. "An unjust law," he noted, "is a code that a majority inflicts on a minority that is not binding on itself. . . . On the other hand, just law is a code that a majority compels a minority to follow that it is willing to follow itself."

He demonstrated that there are instances when a law is just on its face but unjust in its application. "For instance," he said, "I was arrested Friday on a charge of parading without a permit. Now, there is nothing wrong with an ordinance which requires a permit for a parade, but when the ordinance is used to preserve segregation and to deny citizens the First Amendment privilege of peaceful assembly and peaceful protest, then it becomes unjust."

Martin's question today would be whether our immigration laws and policies—either vigorously enforced or tacitly ignored—are inherently unjust. Do they violate God's law?

The answer to that would have to be no, even if viewed only through the context of rendering unto Caesar that which is his domain—in this case, the protection of borders. Martin, I think, would consider the only injustice to be the law's practical application that favors those who have managed so far to evade arrest—that is, almost everyone here illegally—and puts anyone who chooses to go through legal channels at a practical disadvantage by dropping him into a labyrinthine bureaucracy more overburdened and inept than if it were run by the Three Stooges. As it stands, our legal-immigration apparatus recalls an old Soviet joke about a woman who buys a washing machine and is told it won't arrive until June 5—eight years later. "Morning or afternoon delivery?" the clerk asks. "Better make it morning," says the woman. "The telephone guy is coming that afternoon." With politicians of both parties—and a president of either party—willing to grant amnesty for illegal aliens and offer a path to citizenship, there's no reason why those who want to come to America should not expect that breaking the law will eventually be rewarded.

The United States is still considered the ultimate land of opportunity, which, after all, is the reason so many illegals flock here. That speaks well of us. Anyone in the world is free to apply for admittance, then residency, then citizenship to the United States. And of the millions who do play by the rules—even if it takes decades, as it often does—about 700,000 a year satisfy the requirements to be granted citizenship, many of them, it should be noted, with black skin from the Caribbean and West Africa who in a single generation acquire admirable fortunes through brains and hard work. That, too, speaks well of us.

Meanwhile, the U.S. government offers another 50,000 people permanent-residence slots through an annual lottery open to citizens of countries that have not typically sent emigrants to the United States.

In short, Martin would conclude, there's nothing inher-

ently racist about immigration policy or the laws that gov-
ern it, and while it's true that immigrants from anywhere
with at least a million dollars to invest on American soil are
granted immediate entry and permanent residency, he'd say
that that strategy seems entirely reasonable, if only because
anyone who can offer opportunities to others serves the
public good.

So now Martin would ponder the broader question of
whether immigration policy is innately immoral. He'd ask,
"Should people of every country have the right to live in
every other country?" (Singling out the United States as a
special case would be both unfair and immoral.)

Though he sometimes spoke in grand philosophical
terms of moving beyond national borders to become a one-
world nation or a one-nation world—sentiments described
in more fairy-tale terms by John Lennon in "Imagine"—
Martin remained cognizant that earth was not heaven;
there were no actual utopias, no countries led by perfect
governments or benevolent tyrants. And anyway, if we did
all join together as one nation, by whose laws would we be
governed? Saudi Arabia's? Sweden's? And who would make
that determination? Chileans? Vietnamese?

What Martin dreamed of and worked for was a country
that abided by its Constitution in letter and spirit, a country
that lived up to its stated principles. Such a country's virtues,
he said, would provide opportunities that make it the greatest on earth for *all* of its citizens, not just *most* of them.

As such, he recognized that the United States had the
right—and particularly after 9/11, he would agree, it has
the obligation—to protect and safeguard its citizens not
just from terrorist attacks but against any actions of preventable violence from those who want to come here by
any means necessary and do harm to innocents, possibly

in conjunction with street gangs. The hyper-violent MS-13 gang (Mara Salvatrucha), for example, composed primarily of illegals from El Salvador with franchises across the country, is presumed by intelligence agencies to be smuggling Al Qaeda terrorists into this country. That means it is not facile to believe that violence can be reduced by keeping out those not legally entitled to be here, if only because just by being here they are, by definition, breaking the law.

The sheer numbers of illegal immigrants on these shores has spawned several cottage industries, including de facto networks of suppliers for false documentation and identification. If you don't look too much like a cop—or even if you do—you can probably get a driver's license from whatever state you want and a passably authentic Social Security card by showing up wherever the "undocumented" gather and paying the going rate. At least four of the September 11 hijackers went through those channels for the IDs that got them onto the planes that they turned into missiles.

Consider, too, what happened in the late summer of 2007, on the playground of an elementary school in Newark, New Jersey, where four friends—friends since they'd attended this school years before—were hanging out and telling stories of back when and sharing excited dreams of the future. And why not? They'd made it; they'd survived one of the most dangerous cities in America, had stayed out of gangs and trouble and kept to their studies and graduated from high school and were heading off the following week to college, Delaware State University. Alas, that wasn't to be.

The four were assaulted, robbed, forced to kneel, and shot in the head at close range, execution style. Three died. That the fourth, a young woman, survived was merely a lucky accident; it sure wasn't for lack of intent. And her incredible strength helped the police find the assailants—several teenagers, a man in his mid-twenties from Central America, and a man in his late twenties, José Carranza, a Peruvian national who turned out to be the shooter. All were—or had been—illegal immigrants until the Department of Immigration and Customs Enforcement offered them, as citizens of Honduras, El Salvador, and Nicaragua, what's called Temporary Protected Status—a designation that can only be lost by conviction of a felony or *two* misdemeanors.

This has the net effect of giving those with TPS a get-out-of-jail-free card even when they're caught in a gang sweep targeted at street gangs like MS-13.

Not even the thirty-one-count indictment filed earlier against Carranza for aggravated sexual assault of his girlfriend's 5-year-old daughter over a two-year period—meaning she was 3 when he started molesting her!—and then threatening the girl's parents with physical harm was enough to keep the arraigning judge from issuing him bail, just as when Carranza was later arrested on assault charges for a bar fight.

More astoundingly, neither were those charges considered grievous enough to attract the attention of the immigration authorities. Would they have acted on the information and targeted him for deportation? We'll never know. Were they even notified? Probably not.

Newark, like New York, like Los Angeles, like too many American cities, big and small, has designated itself a "sanctuary city" in order to keep local law enforcement from inquiring into a suspect's legal status. The designation—a collusion between business interests, illegal alien activist groups, and politicians—was designed originally as a way to keep Officer Smith from contacting the immigration feds after nabbing gardener José innocently jaywalking across Elm St. on the way to Mrs. Simpson's rose bushes. Instead the issue has devolved to the point where the city of Los Angeles, among others, stopped impounding the cars of drivers who are found to have no license—not, no license on them, as in forgetting to take a wallet, but no license issued by the Department of Motor Vehicles. This, of course, mostly pertains to illegal immigrants, who are prevented by law from obtaining licenses that pass legal muster when checked against a database. But then the Ninth Circuit Court of Appeals ruled that impounding the vehicle of someone who's not legally supposed to be driving it, let alone entitled to be in this country, actually violates the Constitution's protections against unreasonable search and seizure. That led some city attorneys to err on the side of prudence rather than face possible lawsuits from illegals. So the only cars towed were those that belonged to licensed drivers—that is, those carrying *valid* licenses issued in good faith by the Department of Motor Vehicles to United States citizens or legal residents.

This is where Martin Luther King would throw up his hands and wonder why he had to point out the immorality of the laws as practiced, not as written; and of the moral brazenness of those without the legal right to be here who demand that Americans treat them as though they were decorated soldiers or fighters for constitutional rights. To him, breaking the law meant paying the price for it. Willingly and gladly. Even voluntarily. Anything less was dishonest, ignoble, and unworthy.

What would Martin say to illegal aliens? He'd say, "If you're in this country illegally, have you come here in order to protest what you consider an 'unjust law'? If you haven't, then for whatever other reason you're here, even if it's to make money for your sick child, which is as good a reason as there is, then you're just violating the immigration laws of this country and deserve no more consideration from the authorities than does a thief. If you choose to stay here, I hope that you'll come out of the shadows and apply legally and then jump through whatever hoops that entails, just as I would have to if I wanted to remain in your country without breaking the law. And should that lead to your deportation, I hope charitable people of means will help your child financially. For as long as you're here, though, you should know that I find it offensive and insulting when you wave Mexican and Salvadoran flags and compare yourself to civil rights demonstrators—black American *citizens*—who were denied their inalienable rights as Americans by those who hated them only and entirely because of their skin color. Given that you weren't born here, as opposed to descending from people who'd been dragged here in chains, how is your situation—choosing to sneak across a border, sometimes paying a *coyote* thousands of dollars to get here—reminiscent of theirs? You hold up signs demanding rights that you insist are yours by virtue of being here and working here, which is something like my stealing your car and feeling entitled to own it because I filled the tank with gas. You claim that the United States owes you. But why? Why do you expect to enjoy more rights in my country than I would have in your country? And why when you don't get those rights do you accuse my country of corruption and cruelty? Why are Americans who expect you to play by the rules—just as they have—racist, even though it's clear that almost all Americans welcome immigration from around the world, particularly if it's legal? And by the way, if *they're* racist, then what word is left for the Bull Connors of the world? Do you expect the United States to open its doors to anyone who wants to come from everywhere in the world—that includes 2 billion Chinese and Indians—or should it open the doors only to your people? What do you propose to exchange for the free education and medical care given to your children courtesy of American taxpayers? Why are you not demonstrating in your own country for political change and jobs that offer a reasonable wage and opportunity for all? Where I come from, we call that having a lot of nerve.

"But to those of you who *did* come to this country illegally in order to protest what you believe to be unjust immigration laws, I ask: Why do you not make your presence known to the authorities and the media and the public so that you can be arrested in front of as many eyes as possible, and then deported for all the world to see? Wouldn't that be a more effective and moral protest than your repeated demand for instant legalization? Might not mass deportations galvanize the American public's support for you, so that rather than calling their members of Congress to urge votes against amnesty, Americans will insist that their representatives vote for you to stay, just as they quickly began supporting civil rights for blacks after they saw them beaten on the Edmund Pettis Bridge. That's how the civil rights movement that I led succeeded, the movement you claim to be carrying on—by repeated acts of civil disobedience against immoral laws and policies. Frankly, what you're doing now I'd call *un*civil disobedience."

That's what Martin would say. But that wouldn't be all he'd have to say.

To Elvira Arellano, he'd say: "Young lady, you keep talking about establishing 'immigrant rights.' What you really mean by that is granting the rights of *legal* immigrants to *il*legal immigrants. Please understand and appreciate the difference. You sneaked into this country and we do not owe you that which you desire, in the same way that a burglar isn't entitled to a nice meal and a slice of homemade apple pie for dessert from someone whose jewelry he's about to steal. I've noticed that, unlike most immigrants who come here legally, you seem to have no affection for this country, or if you do it's hidden behind a litany of complaints. You talk about what you should be given as opposed to what you can earn, as when you spoke at that press conference in Tijuana after your deportation and criticized the way the United States treated you. Why did you not instead say thank you to this country for making your son a citizen and giving him an education and paying for your medical care and his? Not a word of gratitude passed your lips. That makes you, you should know, look like the kind of person most people here aren't sad to see go. Anyway, it's strange to me that Mexicans, unlike the white Europeans who fled to America for opportunity in the last centuries, seem often not to embrace their new country; they appear to feel that this country is less a home than a place of employment. Too often, it seems, they show greater allegiance to Mexico—even waving the Mexican flag at rallies and demonstrations while demanding rights *in the United States*. I can tell you, as a veteran of the civil rights movement who paid the ultimate price, that this is not the way to win the hearts and minds of Americans. If you come here with your hand out, don't be surprised when it gets slapped shut."

To politicians who pander cravenly to the illegal immigration lobby, he'd say: "You were elected to do what's right by your American constituents, whether or not they line your pockets with reelection donations. Please, before you make it easier for the unfortunate of other countries to come here, consider the cost of your actions on the less fortunate of the country whose Constitution you've sworn to uphold."

To businesses who knowingly hire illegal aliens or choose not to know, Martin would say what he preached to the congregation at Ebenezer Baptist while still a student. He'd say,

"We do not have to look very far to see the tragic consequences which develop when men worship the almighty dollar. First it causes men to be more concerned about making a living than making a life."

To black Americans who have seen their jobs taken, and schools overtaken, he would say: "Why have you stood silently and turned the other way as though the fight belonged to someone else and not you, and the damage being done was not harming you?"

And to the leaders of the black community who claim to have the interests of their people at heart, he'd say: "Brothers, if half a dozen white men had executed some of our young black brothers, you would have been on the next plane and turned this mass murder into a 24/7 cable news show, each of you trying to outdo the other with purple rhetoric about how racist America still is and how even young African Americans who keep their noses clean and play by the rules will have their dreams shattered and their families destroyed by the ineradicable virus of white racism. Why are you silent now? Why are you not organizing protests in Newark, insisting that the city council and the mayor and the police rescind the city's sanctuary status? And why aren't you doing the same wherever young men who have no legal right to be in this country gun down young black men whose ancestors have been on this soil for hundreds of years. In other words, why are you not in *every* city insisting that the police be allowed to enforce the laws? How many pieces of silver from political grievance groups that advocate for illegal immigration has it taken to buy your silence? Oh, and how much extra does it cost for you to do nothing when your people lose their jobs?"

FIVE

WHAT WOULD MARTIN SAY ABOUT ANTI-SEMITISM?

A FEW WEEKS BEFORE HIS ASSASSINATION, MARTIN Luther King was invited by a close friend to a Catskill Mountain hotel for a birthday party. The Catskills are known—or used to be, anyway—as the place where middle-class New York Jews of the 1950s and '60s spent their summer vacations, staying in resorts whose entertainments catered to their cultural tastes, especially comedy. If you've ever heard the term "Borscht Belt comedian"—for example, Buddy Hackett, Henny Youngman, Shecky Greene—you know what the Catskills were. So not surprisingly, the close friend who invited Martin to celebrate his sixtieth birthday with him was Jewish. But not just any ordinary civilian Jew, if you will. This was Abraham Joshua Heschel, professor of Jewish ethics and mysticism at the Jewish Theological Seminary in New York, one of the most prominent and accomplished Jewish thinkers in America—a man whom Martin considered to be one of his closest and most assiduous supporters, as well as a great friend. Asked why, in 1965, he had left the safe confines of New York to take part in the dangerous voting rights demonstrations Martin led in Alabama, Heschel said, "When I march in Selma, my feet are praying."

Those were the days when blacks and Jews marched arm in arm in the struggle for civil rights, and together sang the civil rights anthem "We Shall Overcome." No wonder. Jews had been the world's most reliably persecuted race for more than two thousand years, a sad and horrible truth that had inspired Winston Churchill to remark that, from the Jew's point of view, all of history is a catastrophe. And though they had largely found a tolerant home in the United States—free from pogroms—for most of American history Jews were still considered outsiders in gentile white society. In Martin's day they were still subject to quotas at elite universities and professional schools; and some industries, like advertising, tried to remain as *judenfrei* as possible until the 1970s.

Most Jews naturally identified with the Negroes' struggle for civil rights. That along with their embedded tradition of philanthropy and charity made them more liberal and open-minded than the average gentile. It's well known, I think, that Jews were instrumental in forming the NAACP back in 1909, and that their financial contributions helped keep the Movement going forward through the decades. The alliance between blacks and Jews was natural and powerful—a fact illustrated painfully by the infamous murders in Philadelphia, Mississippi, of three young civil rights workers who were registering voters during the early summer of 1964. James Chaney was black; Andrew Goodman and Michael Schwerner, who had come from the North to help, were Jewish.

Martin himself often compared American Negroes to the Hebrew slaves, a common allusion in black life since Africans were introduced to the Bible. Both Negroes and Jews, he said, remained psychologically enslaved even after deliverance. "Almost twenty-eight hundred years ago, Moses set out to lead the children of Israel from the slavery of Egypt to the freedom of the Promised Land. He soon discovered that slaves do not always welcome their deliverers. . . . They would rather bear those ills they have . . . than flee to others that they know not of."

Indeed, Martin said, the story of the Exodus was "the story of every people struggling for freedom."

And as late as the day before his assassination, this modern Moses declared in Memphis—named for the ancient capital of Egypt!—that he had "been to the mountaintop" and to "the promised land" but that he "may not get there with you." (An interesting irony is that Martin was the greatest orator of modern times, while Moses suffered from a speech impediment and needed his brother Aaron to speak for him.)

Martin was moved not merely by the obvious parallels between Hebrew slaves and black slaves, and pogroms and lynch parties, and how each group had been uprooted from its homeland. More, the success that Jews had achieved in America was what he desired for Negroes, and their prescription for success was one he wanted to write for his own people: unwavering commitment to excellence and intellectual vigor. That was something he admired, once pointing out to me that, in synagogue, congregants rise only to honor the Torah—written words—as it's removed from or returned to the ark; no human being, not even Moses, is so honored. (Temples often invited him to speak during Friday night Sabbath services, knowing that they could pack their usually half-empty houses of worship, and Martin happily accepted, eager to speak before a friendly audience

and knowing that he could leave with some hefty donations for the Movement. "I consider you real friends of our
struggle," he would say.)

No matter how devastated their communities may have
been by enemies who wanted to destroy them almost every
generation, in a single generation or less Jews would succeed
again. This is what Martin intended for his own people, and
he believed that it was possible. Call it a shared dream.

During the 1930s, Rabbi Heschel personally had
watched the Nazi nightmare unfold, with Jews losing their
rights and freedoms day by day, before fleeing Poland in
1939 just before the German invasion. He told Martin that
the treatment of Negroes in the South reminded him of
how Nazis treated Jews in the Warsaw ghetto. Asked by
President Kennedy to attend a convocation of religious
leaders on civil rights, the rabbi responded by telegram:

> Please demand of religious leaders personal involvement
> not just solemn declaration. We forfeit the right to wor-
> ship God as long as we continue to humiliate Negroes.
> Church synagogue have failed. They must repent. Ask of
> religious leaders to call for national repentance and per-
> sonal sacrifice. Let religious leaders donate one month's
> salary toward fund for Negro housing and education.

Heschel had asked Martin to deliver the keynote address
at his birthday celebration in the Catskills, which was actually
a convention of the Rabbinical Assembly of America. When
the two men entered the ballroom arm in arm, a thousand
conservative rabbis immediately stood, locked arms, and
swayed in unison as they sang "We Shall Overcome"—in
Hebrew. You'd get a lump in your throat if you saw a scene
like that in a movie. I get one just thinking about it.

To be sure, Martin could never tell that story without being visibly moved by the memory. I heard him refer to it a dozen times in what would be his last year—how he'd kidded "Brother Heschel about his ancestors surely coming over on one of those slave ships with us."

Not for the first time, though, did I hear him say how the Jewish community's support had been "simply amazing."

He instructed me, "If any of our folk start talking about 'Black Power' or they disparage the commitment of our Jewish brothers and sisters to our movement, just tell them about that experience in the Catskills. There isn't anyone in this country more likely to understand our struggle than Jews. Whatever progress we've made so far as a people, their support has been essential. Any black person who engages in or supports anti-Semitism needs to know about my reception in the Catskills."

It was disheartening to Martin that so many blacks could be influenced by Elijah Muhammad's Nation of Islam and other black separatist movements to not only reject Martin's message of nonviolence, but rumble and grumble about Jews and "Jew landlords" and "Jew interlopers"—even "Jew slave traders." If the idiom had existed then, Martin would have invoked "No good deed goes unpunished" as an explanation for the black backlash to the depth and breadth of Jewish support. For miserable and familiar reasons, that support and the people who offered it were being met with a measure of resentment and anger that have, in many ways shamefully, grown over these four decades.

Early in 1968, Martin spoke at Harvard and afterward answered questions. One of the questioners asked him about Zionism—the movement to reestablish a Jewish nation in the ancient homeland of the Jews. At the time, embers were still cooling metaphorically after the Six-Day War between

Israel and three Arab states; unquestionably, and much to the surprise of Arabs and the world, the war demonstrated Israel's military superiority. Despite winning a defensive war launched specifically to destroy it—the genocide of all genocides—Israel had since offered to give back land captured in that war. The Sinai Peninsula and Gaza Strip from Egypt, Golan Heights from Syria, and West Bank from Jordan were all offered in exchange for nothing more than recognition of the Jewish state's existence. But the offer had been rejected out of hand, as it would be frequently in the decades to come.

Quickly, segments of the American left that included black militants began to view Israel not as some plucky little state built on desire but as an illegitimate usurper of the oppressed third world, which was why Martin could see that the questioner's hoped-for response was condemnation of the Jewish state.

He could have, if he'd chosen to, begun by quoting W. E. B. Du Bois, who in the early twentieth century wrote that the "African movement means to us what the Zionist movement must mean to the Jews."

Instead, Martin responded pointedly. "When people criticize Zionists," he said, "they mean Jews. They are talking anti-Semitism." The oldest "ism" in recorded history.

Today, black-Jewish relations are not what they used to be, and for that Martin would place fault primarily on the shoulders of black leaders—for making anti-Semitic statements, inciting anti-Semitism (including violence), and failing to condemn overt anti-Semitism within the black community, which has the net effect of allowing it to spread like a disease, as if passed by unwashed hands. Young black people—actually, blacks of any age—who harbor feelings of anti-Semitism need to know about far more than Martin's reception in the Catskills. They need to know that Martin himself would be appalled by their feelings and point out that they seem to be motivated by envy, ignorance, and racism.

Not for nothing is envy one of the deadly sins. And not for nothing did the commandment not to covet your neighbor's anything make God's top ten.

"Negroes," Martin said, "nurture a persistent myth that the Jews of America attained social mobility and status solely because they had money. It is unwise to ignore the error. . . . In a negative sense it encourages anti-Semitism and overestimates money as a value. In a positive sense, the full truth reveals a useful lesson. Jews progressed because they possessed a tradition of education. . . . The Jewish family enthroned education and sacrificed to get it."

To Martin, who believed the pursuit of excellence would trump adversity, Jewish success should, and could, be used as a blueprint and inspiration for blacks to commit themselves to the pursuit of excellence, rather than as an incitement to bitterness.

When American cities were burning in the summers before he died, Martin listened to any number of young blacks who'd been holding matches blame Jewish landlords or Jewish store owners in the inner city—no matter that Jews were anyway a minority of landlords and store owners. It grieved him to hear his people talk like the two little pigs who had casually built their houses of straw and twigs, only to complain how it wasn't fair that their brother had taken the time and effort to construct his house of bricks.

If you're going to focus on Jews, Martin asked, why not wonder who else might have bought the buildings that we lived in and rented us apartments? Who else was willing to come in and open stores and sell us the things we needed?

If Negroes had been in a position to buy those businesses and buildings, why hadn't they done so in the first place? Where were those Negroes with money who'd abandoned their communities? And if blacks *had* bought those businesses and buildings, would they have charged less for rent and bread and taken better care of the premises than the Jews who'd actually lived in the neighborhood before it became a Negro ghetto? Hadn't landlords, including Jewish landlords, taken their cues about how to treat the properties from the often contemptuous way tenants treated their own residences?

Watching the buildings go up in flames, Martin predicted that it would be a long time before significant investment capital found its way back into the inner city. In Los Angeles, for example, it took more than forty years after Watts burned before another supermarket chain took the financial risk of coming back—forty years that included the Rodney King riots of 1992. Residents had to travel miles by bus or car into other neighborhoods to do their shopping at an affordable price. (In the interim, Koreans had become the new Jews, the object of scorn, derision, and contempt for operating the businesses that blacks frequented.)

Jews made a convenient target, just as they had for two thousand years, though now the ones shooting arrows their way were black. At the time, two decades after World War II, those Jewish children born in the Depression to the wave of Jewish immigrants who'd come to America penniless in the early twentieth century were at last bearing the financial fruits of their culture's emphasis on the pursuit of excellence and education.

It's true that Jews had the advantage of looking white—most of them, anyway. (There are between 50,000 and 150,000 self-identified black Jews in the United States, according to demographer Gary Tobin.) They could change their name and, if their noses weren't too big or their hair too curly, pass in white society.

Blacks, on the other hand, were prisoners of their skin color. Even so, Martin, who loved parables, would have considered their gripes sour grapes over the fact that Jews had literally worked their way out of the old neighborhoods, leaving blacks to move in.

Then, too, there was ignorance. Not just historical ignorance, either, but ignorance of economics—the idea that the pie had only so many pieces, and that therefore someone's great big slice meant that someone else was getting less or none. This zero-sum calumny was the Big Lie that black demagogues were selling to the black masses. Jews, it was alleged, were getting fat off the sweat of Negroes, just as plantation owners always had. Jews were taking what rightfully belonged to others. Jews were bloodsuckers, diamond merchants, clannish, cliquish, selfish—all the usual slanders associated with anti-Semites' view of Jews.

Of course, the more ignorant one is, the bigger the lie one will swallow. So when black nationalist demagogues in New York like Daniel Watts began pointing an angry finger at Jews for decrepit conditions in Harlem, home to most black New Yorkers, they chose history's most reliable scapegoat—the one that never seemed to require facts or context before being adjudged guilty.

Watts was publisher and editor of *Liberator*, a black nationalist magazine that counted among its contributors James Baldwin and actor Ossie Davis until the Jew hatred grew too virulent. "I think it is immoral to blame Harlem on the Jew," Baldwin said, knowing that Jews had long ago lived there and still owned many of the apartments that rent control laws made impossible to maintain better, particularly when residents themselves showed little pride in the premises.

But Watts found a willing audience in the growing black nationalist movement that could not have prospered without the usual suspects to blame. As *Time* put it in 1967, "Ever since it was founded in 1960, *Liberator* has been building up to anti-Semitism. From white-baiting, it passed to the baiting of moderate Negroes and finally to Jew-baiting. Jewish merchants exploit Harlem Negroes, screams *Liberator*; Jewish liberals have sold out the civil rights movement."

Liberator never had a circulation higher than fifteen thousand, but there were many other magazines like it in cities across the country purveying a similar message: that white men in general, and Jews in particular, were the devil. In time such secular demagogues merged with or were usurped by the potent blend of black self-reliance and religion offered by Elijah Muhammad's Nation of Islam. Malcolm X (the X in place of the unknown African name his forebears couldn't pass on to him) had been perhaps the most prominent adherent of the NOI until his epiphany at Mecca led him to leave the black Muslim sect. He then disclosed that Elijah Muhammad had violated his own teachings by, among other things, impregnating his teenage secretaries.

This infuriated the NOI, and especially Louis Farrakhan, who had by then given up his career as a calypso singer and become Malcolm's protégé, which in essence made him third in line for Elijah Muhammad's ministry. Well, he was now second, but he knew the damage that these revelations could do to the Nation, coming from someone so prominent. He called Malcolm a traitor and preached that his actions "were worthy of death"—words that led, in early 1965, first to the firebombing of Malcolm's house and then to his assassination at a hotel ballroom in front of his wife and children by at least three NOI members; three, anyway, were convicted.

Martin was in Selma at the time of the assassination and we immediately stepped up security around him, though of course for him the threat came not from *black* segregationists but from *white* segregationists.

Three days later he arrived in Los Angeles for "Martin Luther King Days," as voted by the L.A. City Council and County Board of Supervisors, and had to give an impromptu press conference at the airport. "Well," he said, "I think we must face the fact that there are some very ghastly and nightmarish aspects of violence taking place at this time, and it does seem to be a feud between some of the black nationalist groups."

The secondary tragedy, Martin said, was that Malcolm's death came at a time when he was "reevaluating his own philosophical presuppositions and moving toward a greater understanding of the nonviolent movement and toward more tolerance of white people, generally." Including Jews.

The writer Nat Hentoff recounts an incident that occurred at a New York college where Malcolm was speaking a year before his death. During the question period, a black student rose and began attacking Jews—all Jews, past, present, and future—with practiced viciousness. Malcolm wouldn't let him finish. He grabbed the microphone and, as Hentoff wrote, "with the icy anger his critics knew so well," said, "What you're doing is what has for so long been done to us. Bigotry doesn't help anybody, including the bigot. Listen, I don't judge a man because of the color of his skin. I don't judge people because they're white. I don't judge you because you're black. I judge you because of what you do and what you practice. I'm not against people because they're Jews. I'm against *racists*."

Alas, this was not the message heard long enough from those of his followers—and those of the Nation of Islam—who confused hatred with liberation. No wonder Martin wrote a *Wall Street Journal* obituary lamenting that "the murder of Malcolm X deprives the world of a potentially great leader." Addressing himself to "the young men of Harlem and Negro communities throughout the nation," Martin wrote, "We will still suffer the temptation to bitterness, but we must learn that hate is too great a burden for a people moving on toward their date with destiny."

But hate often seems to be a fashionable crowd-pleaser sold, directly or not, by some black leaders today, and I don't think I have to tell you what Martin would say about that. Even so, to fully appreciate his sentiments, it would be helpful to review some of the actions regarding anti-Semitism by three of the more prominent black leaders, Rev. Jesse Jackson, Louis Farrakhan, and Rev. Al Sharpton.

In 1984, When Jesse Jackson was running in the Democratic presidential primaries and referred to Jews as "Hymies" and New York as "Hymietown," the initial outcry from those around him was first to deny it and then to focus their ire on the black journalist who had reported the remark, a remark Jackson presumably considered popular and accepted among blacks at the time, there being no whites around (which, if you think about it, seemed to transform legitimate "black pride" in his candidacy into another kind of racism, the assumption that the reporter would automatically be on the same team and want Jesse to win solely because they were the same color). The journalist received more opprobrium from the black community for snitching, as it were, than Jackson did for the insult, something unimaginable if the situation were reversed—if, say, the liberal Jewish mayor of New York, then Ed Koch, had referred to

Mississippi as "Darkieville." Koch would have been forced to resign from office that day, driven out by most of the million or so Jewish New Yorkers who'd have been mortified by the affront. It was Farrakhan, with a history of anti-Semitic preaching—including calling Judaism a "gutter religion"—who regrettably set the tone by publicly threatening the reporter's life instead of chastising Jackson.

But of course Jackson himself now faced a no-win situation. He couldn't distance himself too far from Farrakhan and still retain whatever political viability he still had with his base constituency—militant blacks and white liberals, many of whom, ironically, were Jewish. His "apology" was quickly accepted by Jews, and other black leaders remained silent, either as a tip of the hat to Jackson's prior achievements or because of an all-for-the-team mentality. Even today, the mainstream press, possibly out of racist condescension, continues to run to Jesse for comment and ignore other accomplished African Americans who might have even more valuable insights and advice to provide. This serves to legitimize him among blacks who might otherwise look elsewhere for leadership, needed or not; Jesse, they know, can get face time on TV when he wants, and that gives him power.

Al Sharpton's political rise, like that of his one-time mentor Jesse Jackson, has been the outcome of some masterful manipulation, a sense of excellent timing, and first-class oratory. The rewards, financial and otherwise, seem to have long since overridden whatever remains of that original authentic spark to do good by being good. His first big break came when three black men were chased and beaten by whites in the Howard Beach area of Queens. One of the men, trying to run away, was hit by a passing car and died. Sharpton courageously led a march of mostly black demonstrators through the area and endured taunts and racist epithets from the residents.

Real national fame came next when he championed the story of young Tawana Brawley, who claimed falsely that she'd been raped and smeared with feces by white men. The ensuing saga ruined several otherwise good men's lives and cost Sharpton hundreds of thousands of dollars for the slanders he'd committed against the district attorney.

Then, in 1991, Sharpton regrettably appeared to turn a tragic incident into political hay by criticizing the Orthodox Jewish community of Crown Heights in Brooklyn, an area roughly divided between blacks and Jews, and implying that it bore responsibility for the death of a young black boy when a car driven by a Hasidic Jew accidentally jumped the curb and killed 7-year-old Gavin Cato. A mob set upon Jews in the street, and Yankel Rosenbaum, a Jewish scholar who was visiting from Australia, was stabbed to death by a black 16-year-old named Lemrick Nelson. (Though the police caught Nelson minutes later with the bloody murder weapon in his pocket and Rosenbaum's blood on his clothing, a mostly black jury acquitted him and then later celebrated with him. Twelve years later, Nelson confessed to the crime and, ironically, was convicted of violating Rosenbaum's civil rights.)

Urged on by Sharpton, a grand jury investigated and, in fact, found no basis on which to charge the Jewish driver. Even so, Al's repetitive street chant, "No justice, no peace," incited hundreds of blacks to take to the streets and torch Jewish homes, property, and cars while chanting "Jew, Jew, Jew." Regrettably, the principal elected leader in New York—the mayor, no less—David Dinkins, acted too late to defuse the situation that could have theoretically engulfed all of his constituents, or so it seemed to many New Yorkers.

Four years later, Sharpton organized a boycott of Freddy's Fashion Mart in Harlem after the property's owner asked the operating tenant to evict one of its longstanding subtenants, a black record store. "We will not stand by and allow them to move this brother so that some white interloper can expand his business," Sharpton told his gathering crowd. To him, this was racially motivated, pure and simple, another example of greedy Jews taking what belonged to blacks. No matter that the property's owner was a black Pentecostal church, a fact that—well, let's just say that it would've been improbable for Sharpton not to know this. Still, day after day he kept up the nasty chants, and soon one of his followers shot four whites in the store before setting fire to it. In all, eight people died. And Sharpton? No apology, even for the unintended consequences.

But then, it's not compelled. Mainstream reporters too often give him and other blacks a pass on their apparent anti-Semitism because they buy into the frequently stated rationale for it: Israel. That is, Israel's existence on so-called Arab lands is "provocative," they say.

Martin, for one, could see this coming after the Six-Day War in 1967, which was why he warned repeatedly that anti-Semitism would soon be disguised as anti-Zionism. The truth is that Israel is a democracy of about 5 million Jews (including about 100,000 from Ethiopia) and a million Arabs who have greater political freedom than anywhere else in the Arab world. It was not founded on stolen land, and there would be peace tomorrow if today the Palestinians put down their rocks, stones, guns, and bombs. Sadly, if Israel put down its weapons today, tomorrow there would be no Israel.

But the truth has fallen victim to political agendas. Farrakhan in particular has successfully sold a large number of African Americans on the notion that the Nation of Islam represents black authenticity. That makes sense to some: slave masters were Christian; ergo, rejecting Christianity is an act of affirming one's African heritage, as is choosing an Arabic name—say, Abdul. But in making common cause with the world's Arabs, who are primarily Muslim, this emerging part of black culture has imported much of the Arab world's widespread anti-Jewish antipathy. Jews, Farrakhan has said, are "devils"; they belong to a "synagogue of Satan." Jews set up the Federal Reserve, and "the same year they set up the IRS, they set up the FBI."

Buying the NOI's version of Islam as it relates to Jews requires a liberal amount of amnesia, ignorance, and willful blindness. For one, true Muslims don't recognize the NOI as authentically Muslim. If you don't believe that, ask Malcolm X—rather, consult his autobiography.

Second, long before white slave traders from all European countries found there was a buck to be made in stealing human beings from West Africa and selling them to Europe and its colonies, Arabs had, for centuries, been stealing black Africans from East Africa and selling them into slavery all around the world—including Saudi Arabia. Yet Farrakhan and others have long peddled the preposterous lie that most slave merchants were Jews.

Third, black Africans, many of them Christian, continue to be sold into slavery by Arabs; and if they're not being enslaved, they're being murdered. Darfur, anyone? Mauritania? The silence of the black leadership on these issues is heartbreaking.

You can be sure that what's going on now in Darfur would animate Martin twenty-four hours a day. He'd rally public support, address the United Nations, insist on immediate sanctions, speak about it until he had no voice left, fly from country to country, and hector African and European leaders to *act now!* Whatever Jesse and Al and other black leaders have done, it isn't enough—because the murdering is still going on. That's what Martin would say. He'd say, "Whatever you're doing, do more. And do it better."

He'd also caution African Americans that our history of identifying with anticolonial struggles should not be misapplied here and lead to uncritical support of the Palestinians, and he'd point out that that support could be inferred by Jews and others to mean that blacks themselves appear to prefer the familiarity of bondage to the security of hard work and freedom. And finally he'd say that blaming the world's ills on two-tenths of one percent of the world's population is sheer madness.

I often think about the similarities between the so-called "Greatest Generation" that survived the Depression and fought Hitler, and Martin's generation of civil rights leaders. Both fought wars, both made the world safer and better, both died for democracy, and both were survived by generations that, so far, seem less great than their predecessors. I'm not suggesting that either Jackson or Sharpton are themselves anti-Semitic. What I am saying is that as presumptive heirs to Martin's leadership of black America, they have the moral duty to speak and act against anti-Semitism whenever it rears its ugliness. Not doing so only fosters the growth of this kind of garbage in the black community—to the detriment of everyone, blacks most of all.

SIX

WHAT WOULD MARTIN SAY ABOUT ISLAMIC TERRORISM AND THE WAR IN IRAQ?

IN THE 1960S, IT SEEMED AS IF HISTORY WAS BEING made every day. And many days it really was, with the newspaper becoming, as the phrase goes, the first rough draft. Before satellites and the Internet carried real-time images from almost everywhere twenty-four hours a day, newspapers, more than television, brought us the news, thanks to brave reporters and photographers who had a knack for being where news was being made. Or was it that what they wrote and photographed became news just by virtue of being reported and photographed?

In truth, maybe a little of both. But because the technology had self-limiting constraints—the photos were shot on film that had to be shipped or slowly transmitted in black-and-white, and at best the reporter's copy could be called in telephonically—what actually got on the air or in

print was more likely to be genuine news, not the manufac-
tured kind we've become used to. (And news editors back
then had perspective from having survived the Depression
and World War II and Korea.) We didn't suffer through
the constant bombardment of bizarre images and artificial
stories that now fill our modern news cycle 24/7, especially
on cable stations, so our antennae for authentic news were
more acute back then. Today, no one would line up outside
a movie theater to see a feature-length foreign documentary
of strange, peculiar, and stomach-churning human behavior
from around the world, as they did in 1962, when *Mondo
Cane* was a box-office sensation. We've already seen all that
stuff. In fact, we see its equivalent every night.

By any measure, what was happening in the '60s felt like it
had a greater impact, at least to those of us intimately involved
in the civil rights movement. Every day seemed to bring con-
sequential events, if only because our actions and strategies
brought about decisions and achievements, and sometimes
setbacks, which intersected with what we were planning for
tomorrow and the next day and all the days after that.

Take the twenty-four hours that began June 11, 1963, a
day whose repercussions were felt for the rest of Martin Luther King's life—and therefore *our* lives—though he didn't
participate personally in any of the events.

The morning began with Governor George Wallace of
Alabama standing defiantly in the doorway of Foster Audi-
torium at the University of Alabama, blocking the entry of
two black students—Vivian Malone and James Hood—who
were preparing to enter and register for classes and in that
way integrate the school. Wallace, remember, had vowed
throughout his candidacy and at his inaugural that whites
and Negroes would never, never mix in Alabama's public
facilities so long as his cold heart beat. And cold it was. For

the cameras and microphones, Wallace offered his soon-to-be-famous "Schoolhouse Door" speech.

But a few minutes later history was made. Federal marshals showed up to accompany Assistant U.S. Attorney Nicholas Katzenbach, Bobby Kennedy's second in command, and Governor Wallace had to stand down. (It amuses me to think that, a month before, during a contentious meeting with RFK himself, the attorney general had sneered and all but called me pathetically naïve for suggesting that he himself make a grand dramatic gesture against segregation by walking side by side, hand in hand, with black students into the U of A as a way of confronting Wallace directly. Sneer or not, he apparently took the idea, even if he sent someone else in his stead.)

That night, the president of the United States, John F. Kennedy, commandeered the nation's three television networks for his long-awaited speech explaining the moral imperative behind the civil rights legislation he'd soon be sending to Congress. This was the act for which he'd previously forced Martin to distance himself from two favored advisers, Stanley Levison and Jack O'Dell, in order that the Movement in that commie-fearing time not be tainted by association with men FBI director J. Edgar Hoover considered fellow travelers.

In making his larger point, about the righteousness of pursuing equality, Kennedy ended up raising an issue that slipped under the radar of almost all of those watching and listening, but it would end up defining the nation's agenda for the next ten years. That night, Martin and I and everyone watching with us were giddy, because it seemed that history was at last turning our way.

"Today," said the president, "we are committed to a worldwide struggle to promote and protect the rights of all who wish to be free. And when Americans are sent to Viet-Nam or West Berlin, we do not ask for whites only. It ought to be possible, therefore, for American students of any color to attend any public institution they select without having to be backed up by troops.

"We preach freedom around the world, and we mean it, and we cherish our freedom here at home, but are we to say to the world, and much more importantly, to each other that this is a land of the free except for the Negroes; that we have no second-class citizens except Negroes; that we have no class or caste system, no ghettoes, no master race except with respect to Negroes?

"Next week I shall ask the Congress of the United States to act, to make a commitment it has not fully made in this century to the proposition that race has no place in American life or law. The federal judiciary has upheld that proposition in a series of forthright cases. The executive branch has adopted that proposition in the conduct of its affairs, including the employment of federal personnel, the use of federal facilities, and the sale of federally financed housing."

Our elation was palpable. This day in 1963 had been a day of giant steps forward, especially considering it was supposed to have come in 1956, when a federal judge ruled that skin color could no longer be used to deny admission to a public university. So Autherine Lucy began her first day of classes at the University of Alabama—and learned nothing that she hadn't already known about whites all her life. Crosses were burned, rocks thrown, and her car was attacked, leading the school president and trustees to suggest in the strongest terms that she withdraw for her own safety. But now Governor Wallace, considered at the time the greatest of the great white bigots himself, had been made to capitulate, which meant anyone could. Plus, the president of the United States had proved he would risk some political capital in order to do what's right.

Our celebration would have gone on and on had it not been interrupted by horrifying news from Mississippi: Medgar Evers had been assassinated.

I suspect that the symbolism of such dreadful news following so closely and overwhelmingly after euphoria was not lost on a single American Negro.

Evers had been a World War II veteran, landing with his company on Normandy Beach. Later, after trying unsuccessfully to integrate the University of Mississippi himself (its law school), he became the NAACP's first field officer in Mississippi; and, in 1962, he was instrumental in helping James Meredith become the university's first black student. In the weeks before his murder, he'd been investigating the beating and lynching, in 1955, of 14-year-old Emmett Till, an act sure to be seen as uppity and attract the kind of attention dangerous to a Mississippi Negro in 1963. A Molotov cocktail had already been tossed at his home, fortunately injuring no one, and just days earlier he'd been nearly run over by a car as he left the NAACP office in Jackson. Obviously, he'd become a target. But, like James Meredith, Evers showed no fear, and his enemies surely took that audacity as a double-dog dare.

Now he was dead, struck in the back with a bullet from a deer rifle fired from a lot across the street as he stepped out of his car into his driveway holding a box of T-shirts printed with the message "Jim Crow Must Go." It pleased us, though, to hear that he would be buried a hero at Arlington National Cemetery, which just had to gall those fine Americans who didn't consider him either a hero or an American. (A Klansmen and member of the White Citizens Council, fertilizer salesman Byron De La Beckwith, whose fingerprints were on the rifle, was arrested and tried twice by all-white juries. To their credit, I suppose, they didn't acquit him outright, but after two hopeless deadlocks the D.A. declined to retry. It would take thirty years before De La Beckwith would be tried again and this time convicted. Here's hoping he found his just reward, if that's the word, after dying in a prison hospital.)

Martin captured the whiplash sense of jubilation turned to grief during these hours when reporters called on him for comment. "The brutal murder of Medgar Evers," he said, "came as shocking and tragic news to all people of goodwill, especially after such an eloquent and profound and unequivocal plea for justice and human dignity for all people by the president of the U.S. . . . . This event, or this tragic occurrence, should cause all persons of goodwill to be aroused and cause them to be more determined than ever before to break down all of the barriers of racial segregation. . . . I think it will make Negroes more determined. I think it will cause them to see the urgency of this moment, the seriousness of this thing, and I'm sure it will cause them to rise up with righteous indignation."

The next day's *New York Times* arrived with another story that affected Martin profoundly at a time—literally at the *moment*—when his joy and his sorrow had peaked and become inseparable.

The news—just a brief mention on page 3—was this: Three Vietnamese Buddhist monks wearing traditional robes got out of a car at a busy intersection in Saigon, the capital of South Vietnam. One of them, Thich Quang Duc, sat in the street, assumed the lotus position, and with the help of the others doused himself with a canister of gasoline that they'd carried. He then lit a match and over the next few minutes, as dozens of passersby watched, he allowed himself to be consumed by the flames.

David Halberstam, then a *Times* reporter, happened to be there, as did Malcolm Browne, a photographer. It seems unlikely that this would be a coincidence, but either way they were destined to capture the event, and in so doing they instantly put Vietnam on America's radar and changed the debate terms, if not the country itself.

Halberstam would later describe as best he could what the photo showed better. "I was to see that sight again, but once was enough," Halberstam wrote. "Flames were coming from a human being; his body was slowly withering and shriveling up, his head blackening and charring. In the air was the smell of burning human flesh; human beings burn surprisingly quickly. Behind me I could hear the sobbing of the Vietnamese who were now gathering. I was too shocked to cry, too confused to take notes or ask questions, too bewildered to even think. . . . As he burned he never moved a muscle, never uttered a sound, his outward composure in sharp contrast to the wailing people around him."

Browne would later describe the agony he saw on the monk's face, but he concurred that Thich never uttered a sound and remained in his meditative position until the moment his life force ceased.

Owing to the "All the News That's Fit to Print" ethos of the day, the *Times* was among several papers refusing to run its own photograph, though it was widely seen by midmorning in other papers. The short story that ran was actually more about the commotion and demonstration that prevented fire trucks from reaching Thich Quang Duc in time.

Without the gruesome photo, the story might never have made news in America—except, perhaps, as a prurient page in a *Mondo Cane*–type book. But the South Vietnamese government was a puppet of the United States, which made this our business and maybe our responsibility. The details mushroomed into above-the-fold front-page news: Thich was 67, had spent most of his life cloistered, and chose self-immolation as a dramatic means of protesting against the South Vietnamese government's political repression of Buddhists. Americans may not have known much about Buddhism, but political repression had a bad political ring, especially for a president who believed he might just have lost the support of his entire political party in the South.

Indeed, the story quickly evolved into how the United States would coerce President Diem into allowing greater freedom for Buddhists, who had been, among other things, prevented from flying their flags—a revered rite—on even such important holidays as Buddha's birthday. (Early that November, the corrupt and dictatorial Diem would be murdered after the U.S. either engineered or turned a blind eye to a coup by South Vietnamese generals. One doesn't have to be a tin-foil-hat conspiracist to shudder a little when pointing out that, three weeks later, JFK would be dead, too.)

As a student of religion holding a doctorate in theology, Martin Luther King realized immediately that this monk's suicide violated Buddhism's edicts against the intentional infliction of suffering, against violence, and against causing anyone's death, including your own, even if it's intended to halt terrible misery in others. Thich's death moved and affected Martin in ways that, to me, were noticeable and, I think, surprising to him. By the time copycat acts by both monks and nuns followed in the coming months, Martin seemed transformed.

Yes, he understood that these protests, in violation of religious principle, were not strictly speaking directed against the war in Vietnam, which was just then achieving critical mass in terms of commitment, soldiers, and matériel. Still, the notion of choosing self-immolation—a form of death inflicted throughout history as an agonizing punishment, like Torquemada's auto-da-fé—carried a kind of symbolic power that far transcended, in his mind, marches and sit-ins and moral suasion. I believe he judged himself against the monks and considered their acts of protest to far surpass his own total devotion to making sure Negroes were treated as full American citizens. Seeing how quickly JFK moved on Diem after Thich's death made him wonder what more he could do.

This is not to imply in any way that Martin wanted to up the ante, as it were, or abandon nonviolence as the only moral and most effective tool to achieve integration. But it's clear to me that in the emotional turmoil of those days, Martin began sensing that a nasty little war on the other side of the world might have something to do with the Movement. In its way, that affected everything to come.

2

If this preamble to a discussion of Martin's likely position on the war in Iraq, Afghanistan, and against terrorism itself seems lengthy, please understand that Martin Luther King was too smart and too learned and too decent to judge all events by any other yardstick than morality. His was not a one-speech-fits-all position. To him, the context of an action determined its morals. Sex, for example. This highest physical expression of love between people is blissful and righteous when consensual, or horrifying and repulsively evil when performed against the other's will. All actions must be judged by their context—even, he would insist, those that seem otherwise inexcusable.

I don't doubt that if I'd ever left my wife and children in Martin's care and a man broke into the house with evil intent, Martin would have taken whatever steps were necessary to make certain that, when I came home, I would not find my family dead on the floor—and Martin in a chair explaining that he could not, in good conscience, lift his hand in violence against another man. Did I ever raise such a hypothetical situation with him? No. I didn't have to.

Martin was aware that the sixth of God's Ten Commandments handed down to Moses at Sinai—our moral foundation—proscribed murder, not killing per se. As written in Hebrew, not the mistranslation codified by the King James Bible, *lo tirtzach* refers to the act of murder, defined as unlawful and unjustified killing. Had the commandment been written to avoid all killings, it would have said *lo taharog*. In that case, it would thereby prohibit capital punishment, which, whatever else you think about it, is commanded by God throughout the Torah, as well as animal slaughter for food, which was not only not prohibited, but its proper methods were described. So Martin knew full well, having studied the Old Testament with first-rate scholars, that using the Ten Commandments or God himself as an argument against fighting in general would be as intellectually dishonest as quoting Jesus to bolster a prohibition on wine.

That doesn't mean, however, he didn't find war a sacrilege—the failure of men to reach civilized accommodation, usually because some of those men had evil intent, as defined by the Bible itself. He was too young to fight in World War II, but Martin once told Bayard Rustin that he would have been a pacifist. Would he? I don't know.

Rustin himself had been imprisoned during the war, a pacifist convicted of violating the Selective Service Act. Of course, he'd been born in the South in 1912, and had once spent a month on a chain gang for doing what Rosa Parks later became celebrated for. Plus, he was gay, so he didn't have an inclination to fight for freedom over there when there wasn't much of it here for his kind.

But Martin Luther King was not Bayard Rustin. Despite what he said to Rustin, he loved his country, and he knew the difference between a disgraceful lack of civil rights in an otherwise free country and a country fighting for Aryan supremacy. Maybe that's why he never joined a pacifist organization. Germany's unprovoked aggressions and slaughters were well documented and understood as one man's conscienceless delusions of grandeur; and by then Martin had become aware of how brutally Hitler had treated black German citizens from Germany's former African colonies (the lucky ones merely faced sterilization—without anesthetic). So it was inarguable that Germany offered a clear existential threat to free people everywhere, a threat that the long negotiations and endless appeasements of the 1930s had proved would not be resolved without warfare, if only because Hitler himself would settle for nothing less. Clearly, as long as there was another country to conquer, Hitler would try to conquer it and then select which of its citizens would be allowed to live.

That meant soldiers would have to be sent into harm's way—and as he proved countless times from 1956 to 1968, Martin would never have asked others to put their bodies on the line if he wasn't willing to do the same. The Martin I knew could not have lived with himself if others' blood had bought his freedom while he stood in front of an induction center protesting the draft.

Besides, this man who abhorred the black militants' calls for armed revolution took chest-swelling pride in the extraordinary accomplishments of the Tuskegee airmen, those African American fighter pilots who so wanted to serve their country that they were willing to overcome countless racist barriers and indignities. That's important to note, especially for those who believe Martin considered both parties in a war to be equally culpable, the aggressor and the defender. On the basis of my experiences with him, I find it inconceivable that Martin would have been proud if the Tuskegees had flown for the Luftwaffe, helping Hitler to establish his thousand-year reich.

In a long commentary tracing his intellectual growth, Martin's explanation for why he repudiated communism also applies to Nazism, since his primary objection, he explained, was on moral, not economic, grounds—its "ethical relativism." Communists, he said, have "no divine government, no absolute moral order, there are no fixed, immutable principles; consequently almost anything—force, violence, murder, lying—is a justifiable means to the 'millennial' end."

Under communism, like Nazism, he continued, "the individual ends up in subjugation to the state. . . . This deprecation of individual freedom was objectionable to me. . . . To deprive man of freedom is to relegate him to the status of a thing, rather than elevate him to the status of a person. Man must never be treated as a means to the end of the state, but always as an end within himself."

Well said, but by what means does one bring freedom and justice to those who have indeed been relegated to the status of a thing by those for whom the human heart is a mark of weakness and the human head a trophy?

3

When Autherine Lucy had to flee the University of Alabama for fear of her life in 1956, Martin raised the issue in that week's sermon at Ebenezer Baptist Church, noting that the local newspaper described the mood as "quiet" in

Tuscaloosa: "There is peace," he read, "on the campus of the University of Alabama."

True, Martin agreed for sake of rhetorical argument, there was now no violence after Autherine's departure. But the absence of violence was not the same as peace: "Yes, things were quiet in Tuscaloosa," he said. "Yes, there was peace on the campus, but it was . . . peace that had been purchased at the exorbitant price of . . . a vicious mob . . . at the price of allowing mobocracy to reign supreme over democracy. It was peace that had been purchased at the price of capitulating to the forces of darkness. . . . It is the type of peace that is obnoxious. It is the type of peace that stinks in the nostrils of the almighty God."

And yet, for Martin, the cruel inhumanity demonstrated at the University of Alabama in 1956 did not justify reacting in kind. He believed still, he said, that turning a cheek to the bully was the more devastating blow—the equivalent of losing the battle but winning the war.

That wasn't just rhetoric with Martin. He'd had a vision of how to win and make history, and nothing that happened, no amount of cruelty, changed his mind. But it was he who'd used that splendid phrase "an obnoxious peace"— a peace defined by Churchill when he described appeasement as feeding the crocodile so that he will eat you last. History is replete with countries and populations pacified by the fear of imprisonment and torture and death at the hands of tyrants without consciences—worse, an appetite for blood and pain as a means to glory. Just in the last hundred years there've been far too many such men—Stalin, Hitler, Mao, Ceaușescu, Milosevic, Franco, Assad, Amin, Hussein, Pol Pot, and at least a dozen others—to remember without consulting a reference book. These were (and are) men for whom the ends, whether political or religious or ideological, justified barbarism and cruelty. And just as their names will someday be nudged aside by new tyrants, for each of them there'd been many people of goodwill who wanted to feed the crocodile as a way of bringing peace.

An obnoxious peace.

In 1956 Alabama and 1966 Mississippi, Martin understood well that he could accommodate an obnoxious peace with the evil of segregation because he believed that it was only temporary. And he believed that because he knew that the enemy, though of a different skin color, came from a culture defined by the same book as his—the same Good Book. Martin never lost faith that by holding a mirror up to society's brutality of the Negro, that that society, a democracy born of the Judeo-Christian ethic, would eventually be shamed by its disgraceful behavior and fall to its knees in repentance. Time, therefore, was on Martin's side, which in his mind made passive, nonviolent resistance a devastating weapon of war against racism and segregation—in fact, a more devastating weapon than guns, which would have brought retaliation in kind and the moral justification for their use.

This, too, had been Gandhi's advantage. He absorbed the worst the English could offer in the certain knowledge that they were fundamentally a good people, a Christian, God-fearing people, and that their liberal democracy would sooner rather than later demand that the colonial occupiers do the right thing.

But what if, instead of the English, India's masters had been, say, the Nazis? Imagination can't conceive of the Waffen SS caring too much about a few dozen Indians slaughtered by rifles when, as documented, they murdered millions of white Europeans with bureaucratic efficiency. Or how about Stalin, who among other atrocities engineered the long, slow, agonizing starvation of as many as 11 million Ukrainians (a genocide covered up, then justified, by the Pulitzer Prize–winning *New York Times* reporter Walter Duranty)?

In any event, there's no need to imagine what might have happened had the English not been the Indians' twentieth-century masters. The history of India, thousands of years, is a soap opera of war, subjugation, oppression, followed by more war, more subjugation, more oppression. Of all the people, cultures, and then countries to claim India as their own, only the British left voluntarily without military defeat. That is a more significant and relevant fact than is generally cited by those who, like Martin, consider Gandhi's tactic to be a weapon from the hand of God himself. Well, it was—maybe only because it was wielded against an essentially decent, as well as democratic, people . . . who could listen to reports from the British Raj on the radio.

To Martin, "essentially decent" and "Democratic" also described the United States, even from 1956 to 1968, when Americans could watch the depravities of segregation in their own country in their own living rooms on television. It seemed a winning combination that had history in its favor, so he could afford the kind of confidence that came from knowing that victory was inevitable.

In the 1930s, however, pacifists were like the guys who bring knives to a gun fight. It was then that Reinhold Niebuhr, one of Martin's intellectual and spiritual heroes, gave up pacifism after he realized that pacifists inadvertently side with totalitarian aggression, because they do nothing to stop its spread. In the real world, as all of history validates, totalitarians simply roll their tanks over the pacifists and move on to pacify the rest of the population.

Martin read Niebuhr's argument for just war in *Moral*

Man and Immoral Society, and his commitment to pacifism
was shaken. But then, Martin explained, he had a realization of his own: Niebuhr had misconstrued pacifism to be a
form of "passive nonresistance expressing naïve trust in the
power of love" instead of "nonviolent resistance to evil."

When he was confronted by black militants who had
neither his patience nor his faith in nonviolence, Martin
never wavered. The militants considered this a war that
would have to be fought the way wars always had, which
was why Martin would point out that wars had always led
invariably to further wars; it was time to win one without
spilling blood—the blood of the oppressors, that is. This
war would be won with the blood of martyrs.

Malcolm X called that unthinkable. "Any man who puts
his women and children on the front lines is a chump, not a
champ," he said after learning what Martin had planned in
Birmingham, where in 1963 there had been almost twenty
intentionally unsolved bombings of black homes and businesses over the previous six years.

Stokely Carmichael, too, got tired of acquiring justice a
day at a time instead of having right now what should have
been his anyway. "To hell with conscience and morality," he
said, and a lot of people answered amen.

Martin's reply that "power and morality must go together"
sounded less and less appealing to men holding guns, feeling
the illusion of power that comes from a barrel.

How ironic that so many whites still thought Martin's
civil disobedience tactics were too much, too soon, and too
inconvenient—pretty much what the local clergy had argued
after he was arrested in Birmingham for contempt of court
and parading without a permit in an effort to enforce Supreme Court decisions made years before. His "Letter from
a Birmingham Jail" said it all—said that justice on southern

time with southerners deciding how fast was fast was no justice at all. But a *Playboy* interviewer didn't buy it, suggesting
that Martin was making more enemies than friends.

"Violence is both impractical and immoral," Martin insisted. "I've come to see, and I believe with all my heart, we
cannot make the great moral contribution to our nation that
we should make; we cannot win the battle for justice, if we
stoop to the point of using violence in our struggle. It is my
basic feeling that if the Negro succumbs to the temptation
of using violence in his struggle for justice, unborn generations will be the recipient of a long and desolate night of bitterness. And our chief legacy to the future will be an endless
reign of meaningless chaos. Violence is not the way."

Martin Luther King received the Nobel Peace Prize in
1964, a time when it was still the most prestigious accolade
in the world, a legacy of industrialist Alfred Nobel, who felt
so penitent over his invention of dynamite that he endowed
an annual award "to the person who shall have done the
most or the best work for fraternity between the nations,
for the abolition or reduction of standing armies and for
the holding and promotion of peace congresses."

These criteria clearly applied to Martin Luther King.
But they also, in 1939, applied to Neville Chamberlain,
the English prime minister who did everything he could to
avoid fighting Hitler's Germany, coming home from a conference with Hitler waving a signed treaty and proclaiming
peace in our time—a year before Hitler launched the war
that would eventually kill about 50 million. (No Peace Prize
was awarded in 1939, though Chamberlain was nominated,
as was Hitler, just as Mussolini had been in 1935, the year
he invaded Ethiopia, one of the few remaining black African nations not under European colonial rule. Stalin would
be nominated, by the way, in 1945.)

For Martin, World War II was real, and he was by no means unaware of Chamberlain's inadvertent role in ensuring that the war would be fought. But he also knew that he wasn't fighting Chamberlain's enemy. If he had been, then the world today would look far different and history would remember him as it remembers Neville Chamberlain, which is the last thing anyone wants. Even mass murderers have their admirers. But not Chamberlain. No one wants to be remembered as an appeaser. Martin, certainly, didn't.

"Whenever I come," he said, quoting Jesus, "a conflict is precipitated between the old and the new, between justice and injustice, between the forces of light and the forces of darkness. 'I come to declare war on evil. I come to declare war on injustice.'"

Which is why, in that war on injustice, Martin would take a cold, hard look and reevaluate what it takes to win against the ideological enemy that faces us today. It, too, is totalitarian. It, too, is fascistic. It, too, is conscienceless and sadistic and ambitious. And unlike the United States in the 1950s and 1960s, it is neither Democratic, nor decent, nor Christian.

4

Long before April 4, 1967, the day Martin Luther King stood before a massive assembly of clergy and laypeople at Riverside Church in New York to officially declare his opposition to the Vietnam War, he had already raised the issue in numerous speeches and sermons on other subjects, noting that it was immoral to divert financial resources from the devastation of our inner cities in order to devastate cities eight thousand miles away. And for all that time he and his closest advisers (Andy Young, Bayard Rustin, Stanley

Levison, Harry Wachtel, Vincent Harding, Walter Fauntroy, Lawrence Riddick, and me) wrestled with whether he ought to make his position unambiguously public in one grand declaration devoted only and entirely to Vietnam, and in that way grab the country's attention and awaken the moral outrage of its silent majority. No other subject, to the best of my memory, caused as much contentiousness among Martin's advisers.

Martin, of course, didn't need much prodding to speak against the evils of war. "I believe absolutely and positively that . . . if we continue to use these weapons of destruction, our civilization will be plunged across the abyss of destruction."

But generic declarations weren't the same as calling out Vietnam by name. If I had to pinpoint the day that Martin first felt impelled to draw a moral line in the sand and proclaim himself opposed to the burgeoning war in Southeast Asia, I'd say it was when Thich Quang Duc self-immolated. That was 1963, nearly four years before, and as yet we hadn't marched on Washington and heard Martin articulate his dream. Clearly, there were more pressing issues than the war in Vietnam, which seemed at the time, Thich notwithstanding, like something out of the Peter Sellers movie *The Mouse That Roared*—a tiny country declares war on the United States in order to lose and in that way win some Marshall Plan cash.

In the years since, Vietnam had stopped being any kind of joke. Even so, our best argument against Martin's declared opposition still held sway: President Lyndon Johnson's Great Society programs and his sincere commitment to civil rights were more important and vital than his war policies, and his continued support trumped whatever else was going on. Stanley Levison, brought back into the fold slowly after his exile during JFK's last year, was himself adamantly opposed to sending our boys to fight against a country that, unlike Japan or Germany, could not remotely be seen as a threat to our security. And yet, of all Martin's advisers, he argued more forcefully—and convincingly—than any of us that Martin's public opposition to the war would be seen by LBJ as a betrayal and might therefore hurt the Movement.

It was a potent argument, and it became policy until I brought Martin some facts and figures about the war pointed out by Daniel "Chappy" James, the country's first black four-star general (and a former Tuskegee airman). Martin looked at them and immediately regretted his long acquiescence, believing he'd been wrong to obscure his war criticisms inside another agenda—and he immediately moved, as he said in the speech, "to break the betrayal of my own silences." Based on the disproportionately high numbers of young black men dying in rice paddies, it seemed that the war and the Movement were indeed, as Martin had sensed, intertwined all along.

"Perhaps the more tragic recognition of reality," Martin admitted in the speech, "took place when it became clear to me that the war was . . . taking the black young men who had been crippled by our society and sending them eight thousand miles away to guarantee liberties in Southeast Asia which they had not found in southwest Georgia and East Harlem."

It was an extraordinary speech, and a long one, encompassing history and philosophy and idealism, and explaining that the antiwar movement and civil rights movements were actually one. "Even when pressed by the demands of inner truth," he said, "men do not easily assume the task of opposing their government's policy, especially in time of war. Nor does the human spirit move without great difficulty against all the apathy of conformist thought within one's own bosom and in the surrounding world."

To the degree, though, that Martin's impetus for at last speaking out came from those statistics provided by General James, he had based his decision on false information. I don't know whether the numbers had been intentionally skewed or were accidentally miscalculated, but the truth had become, as the cliché goes, a casualty of war. Martin went to his grave believing that blacks were dying in the jungle at rates three times their proportion of the American population, and indeed, it was only recently that I myself learned otherwise. In the 1960s, blacks accounted for 13.5 percent of America's military-ready population by age—and accounted for just about that percent of the dead in Vietnam.

At the time of Martin's speech in New York the antiwar movement had at last reached critical mass, fueled by young men and their girlfriends and families who saw no need to put themselves in harm's way for a country portrayed as a communist domino whose theoretical toppling might change the balance of power on some global game board. That sounded too hypothetical to be believed, especially with the draft on; and it was this growing movement that would, with the added moral weight of Martin on board, convince Johnson a year later to abdicate the presidency— that is, not run for his second full term.

Even the war's most ardent supporters, including President Nixon, who raised the number of ground troops to half a million, never claimed that Vietnam, by itself, posed an immediate danger to the United States; that would have been absurd. But as far as Martin was concerned, what the war did to the Vietnamese was as important as what it did to Americans fighting and dying there. "A genuine revolution of values," he said in the speech, "means in the final analysis that our loyalties must become ecumenical rather than sectional. Every nation must now develop an overriding loyalty to mankind as a whole in order to preserve the best in their individual societies."

The death of a Vietnamese farmer, whether at the hands of the Viet Cong or American soldiers or the North Vietnamese Army or the South Vietnamese Army, was nonetheless a preventable tragedy.

"This call," he said, "for a worldwide fellowship that lifts neighborly concern beyond one's tribe, race, class, and nation is in reality a call for an all-embracing and unconditional love for all mankind."

And it is precisely this sentiment, in this context, that suggests to me what Martin would say about the need to fight Islamic-based terrorism, whether or not it surprises people.

Some years ago I found myself at a cocktail party that would have been otherwise forgettable if not for an argument about violence and self-defense between two men whose voices made overhearing inevitable. At the time, as I recall, a maniac protected by a flak jacket had just opened fire on a Stockton, California, playground full of children, killing five of them and then himself with his automatic weapon.

"It's too bad," the first man said, "that somebody else there didn't have a gun, too." (I quote from memory.)

"Why?" asked the second man.

"So he could've killed the shooter before he killed any other kids."

"That's immoral."

"What's immoral? Killing somebody before he kills someone else?"

"Yes."

"You mean, if you'd been there and could've stopped the murderer with your gun, you wouldn't have done it?"

"No, it's not up to me to decides who lives and who dies."

I suppose it's unfair to say that their voices were loud. The only loud voice of the two was the first man's, arguing for preemptive action. The other guy was as calm as if he'd just come out of a meditation. But by now the first man was really shouting. He grabbed the other guy's wife, pretended to hold a gun to her temple, and said, "You mean to tell me that if I were about to shoot Valerie, your own wife, and the only way you could stop me was by killing me, you wouldn't do it?"

"No, I wouldn't." (I couldn't see Valerie's face, but I imagine that she was none too pleased.)

By now the first man was apoplectic. "Okay, okay," he said, "let's do a hypothetical. Let's say it's August of 1939, and for some reason you've been granted the gift of pre-science, so you know what's going to happen in the world over the next six years. Not only that, but you're in a position to put a bullet in Hitler's brain and stop what's going to happen. So you'll be saving tens of millions of lives of in-nocent people. Not only that, but you can get away with it. It'll be like when Dorothy melted the Wicked Witch and the witch's people were happy. You get away scot-free and save the world. Do you do it?"

"No. It's not up to me to decide who lives and dies."

Over the years I've thought of that exchange from time to time and wondered what Martin would've said to either man, and how he would've reacted on that playground. I think, ac-tually, he would've found truth in both men's arguments but realized that if he were in such a situation, he would have to choose between the most moral of the two actions; indeed, that is what's required of all of us at any given moment. Faced with doing nothing or putting a bullet through the brain of Adolf Hitler in order to prevent the deaths of 50 million people, Martin might say to God, "If not me, then who? If not now, then when?" To which God, seeing Martin pray for forgiveness, might answer, "Martin, why do you think I gave you prescience and put you there with that gun?" (Those who knew Martin best, or who have studied his life and work, might consider my interpretation of his hypothetical choice here to be a kind of blasphemy. But I believe that when squeezed by his otherwise unwavering commitment to nonviolence, he would have chosen the greater morality of preventing so much death and destruction.)

As for the shooter in Stockton, if Martin could've placed himself between him and the children as a shield, he would have done so, even at the cost of his life. But if his only choice was between pleading from afar for the man to come to his moral senses in the name of God and everything that's holy and good and taking him out with a clean shot, would Martin have fired a righteous bullet—then prayed for the murderer's soul? Again, we can speculate that Martin would have seen this as the most moral action. Why? Because, if nothing else, he might have imagined a parallel situation in which another adult tries to explain to him why he'd allowed little Yolanda or Martin Jr. to be shot by a madman instead of stopping him with a well-placed bullet: "It's not up to me to decide who lives and dies."

"Actually, it is," I believe Martin would say. Then he'd add, "When you do nothing in the face of evil, you are indeed deciding who lives and dies."

5

On the morning of September 11, 2001, as New York's World Trade Center towers were falling, and people chose to jump from a hundred stories up rather than be immolated by jet-fuel fire, and the Pentagon was smoking, and United Airlines Flight 93 had become a hole in the Pennsylvania ground, and for the moment there appeared to be fifty thousand or more dead—I found myself wondering about Martin's reaction. We'd weep together, that I knew. But then what? What would he say? What would he do?

As soon as it became clear this had been not the first but just the latest and most devastating attack against the United States by Islamic terrorists—and that more would surely follow if we continued to do nothing—he would have reluctantly accepted that some kind of measured, military response was morally necessary. Doing nothing in 1993 after a truck bomb masterminded by Islamic terrorists went off in the underground garage of 1 World Trade Center with the intention to kill 250,000 hadn't appeased anyone; it had emboldened them, leading to more terror incidents over the next eight years against Americans and U.S. interests in Saudi Arabia, Tanzania, Kenya, and Yemen—all of them planned and financed by Osama bin Laden's Al Qaeda terrorist network.

There had also been Islamist attacks in the Philippines, India, Kashmir, Russia, Chechnya, southern Thailand, Algeria, and so on, and there would be many more ahead: in Bali, Spain, Egypt, England, Holland, and of course, Israel.

The proclaimed goal of Al Qaeda matches the goal of all other Islamist groups: the establishment of a worldwide Islamic state—a caliphate—governed not by democratic rule but by sharia—that is, Islamic law based on the Koran. "We will turn the White House and the British parliament into mosques," an Al Qaeda position paper declared. Or, as Abu Musab al-Zarqawi, Al Qaeda's leader in Iraq, put it, "The attacks will not cease until after the victory of Islam and the setting up of sharia" everywhere on earth.

After September 11, doing nothing and hoping for the best no longer remained a useful option. Nor was negotiation or dialogue even a remote possibility. There was nothing to negotiate or talk about; submit or die had become the only options offered by the Islamists.

"When people see a strong horse and a weak horse, by nature, they will like the strong horse," Bin Laden said exultantly after the attack. "This is only one goal; those who want people to worship the lord of the people, without following that doctrine, will be following the doctrine of Muhammad, peace be upon him: 'I was ordered to fight the people until they say there is no god but Allah, and his prophet Muhammad.'"

Clearly, those who follow Bin Laden and do his bidding were not made of the same stuff as redneck segregationists and Klansmen hiding beneath sheets and trying to create terror anonymously before going back to their jobs as insurance agents and sheriffs. They were not even Vietnamese peasants and soldiers taking up arms on their own soil. These were men willing to die—no, *wanting* to die, *hoping* to die—in a holy war, or jihad, while killing as many non-Muslims (infidels) as possible, preferably women and children, or even the wrong kind of Muslim. Reward for such, they believe, is the eternal gratitude of God (Allah), who proves his pleasure by rewarding the arrival of each martyr (*shahid*) in heaven with seventy-two virgins. Meanwhile, on earth, the martyr's surviving family throws a wedding celebration, handing out sweets to the well-wishers at what's considered the martyr's marriage in heaven.

Bin Laden's 1998 declaration of war against the West was dismissed at the time, to the degree that it was even noticed, as the ravings of a madman, just as the world had yawned at the seemingly laughable plans outlined by Hitler in *Mein Kampf*—proof positive again that liberal democracies are ill equipped to regard seriously the stated aims of those for whom peace, prosperity, and brotherhood are not the ultimate objective. We in the enlightened West assume that all people want what we want, and that if they don't it must be some fault of the socioeconomic dynamic. Talk about provincialism. In fact, Bin Laden and Hitler shared something more powerful than the desire for a beach house and a lucrative retirement portfolio: both dreamed of making the world a garden for their kind only. Hitler sought racial purity; Bin Laden sought Islamic purity.

"The ruling to kill the Americans and their allies—civilians and military—is an individual duty for every Muslim who can do it in any country in which it is possible to do it," Bin Laden wrote, "in order to liberate the al-Aqsa Mosque [in Jerusalem] and the holy mosque [Mecca] from their grip, and in order for their armies to move out of all the lands of Islam, defeated and unable to threaten any Muslim. This is in accordance with the words of Almighty Allah, 'and fight the pagans all together as they fight you all together,' and 'fight them until there is no more tumult or oppression, and there prevail justice and faith in Allah.'"

That kind of Islam described by Bin Laden—dramatically demonstrated by the nineteen hijackers, for whom Bin Laden would take credit three months later while marveling how the successful attacks had brought scores of new devotees eager to follow "the strong horse"—was not the Islam Martin had studied in graduate school, the kind that had transformed the militant, white-hating Malcolm X, after his pilgrimage to Mecca, into a man desirous of kinship and harmony.

Jihadi Islam, Bin Laden's version, glorifies hatred and violence against the western world and its "Zionist-Crusaders" in the belief, apparently, that God enjoys a good murder in His name. For Martin, a man who'd spent his life fighting segregation, the idea of a worldwide apartheid would have been abhorrent, so he could not have even considered accepting as justifiable the Muslim claim that all lands once conquered by Muslims—for instance, Spain—be returned and remain forever Islamic; similarly, that only Muslims are allowed onto Muslim lands with permission; that no Jews ever touch Muslim soil; that reading or carrying the Christian Bible in Muslim lands is a capital offense; that changing your religion from Muslim to anything else ought to bring death; that a Jew in Jerusalem, let alone a Jewish state encompassing Jerusalem, is an unforgivable affront and a cause for jihad.

What would Martin say? He'd say that not all grievances are valid, no matter how loudly they're shouted or repeated. He'd say, just as former British Muslim terrorist Hassan Butt said after a terrorist attack in Great Britain, that seeing westerners blame terrorism on western foreign policy instead of on bad theology makes the *jihadis* "laugh in celebration." He'd say that—just as the white segregationists used to cry about the loss of their way of life made possible, first, by slavery and then by Jim Crow—a Muslim who believes that his duty is only to other Muslims and not the whole of humanity is a Muslim in need of Christianity. Remember, Martin would say, Muhammad commanded his followers to kill their enemies. Jesus instructed his followers to love theirs.

Even an obnoxious peace, Martin would have concluded, may not be possible against such a theology. And just as he did not disapprove of state troopers and the 101st Airborne enforcing the rule of law at the point of a gun in order that blacks be allowed to exercise their civil rights, so, too, would he agree that military action is an unavoidable option that even those who are otherwise committed to nonviolence must be prepared to consider now in order to save many more lives later.

6

In 1996, political pressure forced Sudan to expel Bin Laden from the home where he'd taken up residence—and planned the two U.S. embassy bombings, in Tanzania and Kenya—after the Saudis revoked his citizenship five years earlier. The Sudanese authorities, wanting to get on the good side of the United States, offered him to us, but, with terrorism not yet on our radar, we declined and he became a guest of the ruling Taliban in Afghanistan, a group of thuggish Muslim students and scholars who had seized power over most of the rugged country in 1994 and were imposing a return to the seventh century through means they believed were authorized by Muhammad himself.

It was a perfect fit. The Taliban's version of radical Islam and sharia pleased Bin Laden and his growing army of adherents eager to become martyrs. Afghan women were not allowed to work outside the home, and when they left home they had to be covered head to toe by a burqa; girls could not attend school; widows without means caught begging in the street were beaten by the religious police; all forms of recreation (including kite flying) were prohibited; and the punishments for these, as well as a host of other offenses, including a woman's accidentally showing an inch of ankle, could be stoning, hanging, amputation, rape—all in public, usually on the grounds of a stadium set aside as a torture and killing field.

The civilized world reacted to this barbarism by, in essence, writing a strongly worded letter. Human rights groups, women's rights groups, the United Nations—all protested loudly. While those eloquent and impassioned cries might mean something to diplomats who are little more than bureaucrats, in the real world the Taliban laughed, even when Iran, long considered to have been the world's most oppressive Islamic regime, suggested lightening up a bit. In response, the Taliban staged a grand show, dynamiting masterpiece Buddhist statues 165 feet tall that had been carved into the side of a mountain two thousand years ago. Why did they do it? Because anything not Islamic could not, and would not, be tolerated in Afghanistan.

That was the message Christian missionaries received whenever they tried to enter the country on mercy missions. If they were lucky, death came quickly.

Martin, I assure you, would have long ago led the protests and lent his considerable prestige in order to put Afghanistan's vicious treatment of its citizens atop the world's agenda. Would that have changed anything? Doubtful, as even he'd agree; sometimes the sword is mightier than the pen. Still, the man could not have lived with himself had he remained silent and allowed others therefore to remain ignorant of the evil outside their gated communities and local Starbucks. I can easily imagine him saying, "We Negroes in Alabama and Mississippi asked white folk in New York and California to stand up for us. So we in the United States, all of us, need to stand up for people everywhere who are subject to such repression."

Remember his call for "worldwide fellowship"? His desire to go "beyond one's tribe, race, class, and nation"? His "all-embracing and unconditional love for all mankind"? Long before we began bombing outside Kabul, he would have loudly advocated for the liberation of those millions who'd been subjected to such extreme tyranny—a form of cruel govern-ing that, unfortunately, describes far too much of the Islamic world. Including, as it happens, Saddam Hussein's Iraq.

Martin would have been pleased that our military cam-paign in Afghanistan quickly freed the country from the grip of such evil (alas, guerrilla skirmishes—and sometimes worse—remain to this day and indicate possibly years of fighting ahead). And he would have been thrilled to see the joy of the female population, again venturing out in public, uncovered and smiling; girls attending school and dream-ing of a better future.

Of course, Martin would have been disappointed that the search for Bin Laden goes on. And yet he'd understand that Bin Laden is only one man; his death will not make Islamic terrorism disappear. Only Muslims can do that by embracing moderate preachers offering tolerance and love as opposed to the "strong horse" imams who urge jihad in their mosques every Friday. Which reminds me of an allegorical question I once heard posed to an audience of atheists: "It's midnight, your car breaks down in the worst part of town, and you're terrified. Suddenly, the door to a building opens and out walk a dozen young men. Are you relieved to know that they've just come from Bible study?" Well, I would be. And I know for sure Martin would be. But just as clearly, I know that this man who began his career on the pulpit preaching the morality of nonviolent resistance even in the face of evil would have no kind words for the incitements of Muslim imams who teach that non-Muslims are, as Jews were in Nazi Germany, less than human and therefore to be killed without remorse or second thought.

Take, for instance, Imam Abdullah al-Faisal. "Liberty can never be achieved by democracy," he told his flock at a British mosque in one of several sermons recorded for sale. Some of his other pronouncements are just as chilling: "The way forward can never be the ballot; the way forward is the bullet. Islam was spread by the sword, today it has got to be spread by the Kalashnikov." "You all have to strike against America anywhere in the world you are. Is that clear? You have to learn how to shoot, to fly planes, to drive tanks and you have to learn how to load your guns and to use missiles." "There are two religions in the world today, the right one and the wrong one—Islam versus the rest of the world." "When you have a legitimate target you strike at it. If women and children die they are collateral damage." "You can use chemical weapons to exterminate the non-believer. If you have cockroaches in your house you can spray them, yes with chemicals, chemicals. Who has more dignity, the cockroach or the unbeliever? If you spray the cockroach, spray the Hindu."

It's hardly surprising to hear that among his followers were the so-called shoe bomber, Richard Reid, who tried to blow up a plane and kill hundreds over the Atlantic, as well as three of the men who blew up the London transport system on July 7, 2005—an act of terror that killed fifty-two and maimed many more.

It's also no surprise anymore when Muslims are quoted without shame as saying that, because the infidels offend God, Muslims are empowered to kill as many as they can while crying "God is great." Indeed, *jihadi* websites and DVD shops across the Muslim world offer endless videos of innocents, Muslims and non-Muslims alike, trussed like chickens and slaughtered like lambs, their heads sawed off by whooping *jihadis* for whom the true calling, obviously, is sadism. Some of these murderers caught on video or by cell phone cameras are mere children, and some of the victims are women being stoned. Meanwhile, in Iran, the cameras are present for the public executions of teenagers hanged with piano wire for the crime of being gay.

It should go without saying that the depravities of modern Islam surely aren't practiced or condoned by the vast majority of Muslims, of whom there are 1 billion worldwide. But, Martin would say, as long as that majority provide shelter and silence for the violent and hateful minority, all non-Muslims may rightfully question whether Islam is less a religion than a cult of death—which recalls a point he used to raise about Christians being responsible for other Christians acting like Christians. And for him, it would recall Thich Quang Duc, the Buddhist who protested by immolating himself, not others.

Sadly and despicably, those torturous murders on video might not even have reached the minor-league level for Saddam Hussein, Iraq's leader for thirty years, who killed as many as a million of his own people—men, women, children—most for little or no reason, by methods conceivable only to the most degenerate minds. Yet when the rape rooms, acid chambers, and industrial shredders (men thrown in feet first to maximize their agony) were at last revealed and their living victims debriefed, the world yawned.

The reason, it seems, is that many in the western world have, perhaps ironically, adopted the Arab dictum "The enemy of my enemy is my friend." They consider President Bush their enemy, which made the president's enemy, Saddam Hussein, their friend—or if not friend, exactly, then less of an enemy than such a cruel despot deserves to be.

I'm not certain, frankly, how much faith Martin would have in President Bush's competence. But I am certain that he would not have considered Saddam Hussein his friend. He likely would have stood in front of the world's cameras, calling attention to the Baathist regime's brutality; and I can imagine his going to Iraq and pleading with Saddam to fully open every locked door for the weapons inspectors so that war could be averted. And then I can imagine him, if those efforts proved feckless, feeling no regret when the regime fell.

But what about the war itself?

Martin and his advisers would have pointed out that since the late 1990s the whole of the Clinton administration, including its secretary of state and vice president, had warned of Saddam's reconstituted weapons programs posing a grave threat to the world, including the United States. Hardly a soul in Congress believed otherwise, a sense confirmed by Iraq's unwillingness to allow weapons inspectors complete unfettered access. If Saddam had nothing to hide but everything to lose, everyone wondered, why did he fail to comply with seventeen UN resolutions? Why didn't he give the inspectors the keys to the kingdom himself?

After September 11, those questions had to be answered, at least by the president of the United States, the commander in chief of our armed forces—the man charged by the Constitution with protecting us from attack. As such, he had to weigh the consequences of going to war against the possible consequences of *not* going. That meant imagining scenarios like this one: The United States does not invade Iraq. UN sanctions are soon lifted, which allows Saddam Hussein freedom to continue his weapons program. And years later, several suitcase nuclear bombs are smuggled into the country and explode in Chicago, Seattle, Los Angeles, Washington, and New York.

Forget impeachment. Bush's failure to protect us from such a devastating attack would have had him hanging by his heels from the White House portico before the mushroom clouds had disappeared.

But that would have been too hypothetical a situation for Martin to grant either his imprimatur or his acquiescence to the Iraq invasion, which he no doubt would have considered preemptive, not defensive. Before the invasion, he would, as noted, have done everything in his power to head off the war, including lobbying the president. And it goes without saying that, once the war started, he'd want the killing and bloodshed ended as soon as possible. He'd note the domestic disenchantment with the war and find solace that the majority of his countrymen were demanding peace. He'd listen to generals and military experts on both sides—those who believe the only possible solution is political and those who believe a political solution can be urged along by military action. He'd read the polls and understand that Iraqis do not want to live under occupation any more than Americans do, but that they don't want the United States to abandon the mission until their safety can be reasonably guaranteed. And in recognizing that most Muslim deaths are caused by other Muslims, he'd find ample reason to hope and pray that they can resolve their differences—and he'd recognize that if we left before they do, we would be morally responsible for a bloodbath of historic proportions that would likely result from the military vacuum.

Martin would also note that the United States no longer has a draft, and acknowledge that the brave and heroic soldiers sent to fight in Iraq have chosen to be there; and that they are, by and large, supportive of their mission. He might also observe that we might never have become involved in the first place—and that all Americans, from politicians to ordinary people, would have a deeper perspective on the war—if the military draft had been in place.

Martin would say that if, if, if we and the Iraqis together can succeed in building a stable democracy, it will stand as a model for the rest of the region, and possibly jump-start the reformation that Islam so badly needs if it's to become again one of the world's great religions, creating adherents who believe that God's greatest desire is for His people to treat each other well—whether they believe in Him or not.

And finally, he'd say what he said whenever it seemed that black Americans might never achieve their full civil rights. He said, "When our days become dreary with low-hovering clouds of despair . . . let us remember that there is a creative force in this universe . . . a power that is able to make a way out of no way and transform dark yesterdays into bright tomorrows. Let us realize the arc of the moral universe is long but it bends toward justice."

SEVEN

WHAT WOULD MARTIN SAY ABOUT WHO KILLED HIM?

MARTIN LUTHER KING WALKED WITH PRESIDENT Kennedy through the White House Rose Garden, just the two of them, talking about—what else—civil rights.

It was the late spring of 1963, and each man was worried about different things. JFK's political prospects seemed tenuous; remember, his fateful trip to Dallas that November was made to shore up his support in Texas. He was planning to speak first to the nation about the importance of civil rights legislation and then present Congress with a rights bill—in modern terms, it would have to be considered mild stuff—and at that point he couldn't tell whether it would buoy or sink his presidency. Political polling hadn't yet become a daily tool in Washington, so no one was quite sure how the public was being affected by the television and newspaper reports of the brutality against civil rights protesters down in Birmingham, where the sadistically racist commissioner of public safety, Bull Connor, had turned dogs, guns, fire hoses, truncheons, and bullets on the masses, black and white, assembling in the name of civil rights and desegregation.

In Gandhian terms, the brutality recalled the infamous Jallianwala Bagh massacre in which British Indian Army soldiers opened fire on an unarmed crowd of Sikhs and Hindus, slaughtering as many as a thousand in ten minutes of wanton evil. It's what inspired Gandhi to institute his policy of peaceful noncooperation, believing that unresisted bullets and bullies would eventually shame the Brits into abandoning Indian rule.

In those pretelevision days, it would be nearly thirty years between the massacre and Britain's renunciation of sovereignty. JFK didn't have that long, and neither did Martin Luther King. In America, the protesters were impatient and the segregationists unrelenting. More people of goodwill were outraged every day by what they saw and read, which was why Kennedy felt he needed to do something. But politics came with inherent restrictions.

For his part, Martin had just come off the failed action to desegregate Albany, Georgia, where, in his words, "the mistake" was in overreaching—protesting against segregation generally rather than against a single and distinct facet of it. "Our protest was so vague that we got nothing, and the people were left very depressed and in despair." (Frankly, I'd say the real mistake was neither tactical nor strategic. It was a mistake of naiveté: believing that RFK's Justice Department would enforce the law. In 1961, a Supreme Court ruling had upheld an order of the Interstate Commerce Commission desegregating interstate bus transportation and passenger-station facilities. Our widespread protests against Albany's failure to adhere to the law were no match for the political maneuverings of Mayor Asa B. Kelly and chief of police Laurie Pritchett. Their ally, federal judge J. Robert Elliot, was an unrepentant segregationist who'd been appointed to the bench by JFK in order to shore up his political base in the southern wing of the Democratic party.)

As the action now moved to Birmingham, Alabama, it was not without reason that Martin feared the Movement had actually gone backward. He also sensed that a second failure, in Birmingham, would doom the nation to another hundred years of legal segregation. When dozens of protesters who'd done nothing more than march from Birmingham's Sixteenth Street Baptist Church to city hall were arrested for violating laws that were decided by the whims and caprices of Bull Connor, he felt helpless. We— that is, the Movement—didn't have the money to bail everyone out, so until we got it, we did the next best thing: we got Martin arrested.

It was a surprise to find that the Birmingham city jail offered a solitary confinement cell, but that's where he was put, presumably so that he couldn't incite or organize the other arrested demonstrators. In solitary he was given little access to people or instruments of communication—like a pencil. But he did get his hands on a Birmingham newspaper in which some members of Birmingham's white clergy called him a troublemaker, insisting that the demonstrations for simple human rights were "unwise and untimely." In response, Martin picked up his nut of graphite and, in the margins of that newspaper and on toilet paper, began composing what later became known as the "Letter from a Birmingham Jail."

As his attorney, I was one of the few allowed to see him, and before I left to fly to New York City—where, before my eyes, Nelson and David Rockefeller literally opened the vault to Chase Bank and gave me a suitcase containing $100,000 in cash in order to bail out Martin and as many demonstrators as possible—I smuggled in more paper and some pencils so that he could finish his thoughts for the world to read, then smuggled out the finished pages in my pants.

The words were pitch-perfect. "Frankly," he wrote, "I have never yet engaged in a direct action movement that was 'well timed,' according to the timetable of those who have not suffered unduly from the disease of segregation. For years now I have heard the word 'Wait!' It rings in the ear of every Negro with a piercing familiarity. This 'wait' has almost always meant 'never.'"

Pitfalls and realities were what JFK wanted to talk to Martin Luther King about when they took their walk in the Rose Garden with what seemed like the president's political future and the future of the civil rights movement at stake. Why? Because J. Edgar Hoover, director of the Federal Bureau of Investigation, had just brought some news to the attention of the young president that required immediate attention.

It can be reasonably assumed, and Martin did, that John Kennedy and his brother Robert, who was his attorney general, lived in fear of Hoover, believing that Hoover had enough dirt on either or both of them or the Kennedy family to bury their fortunes with a well-placed leak to the press. Those were not the days when the populace was eager, at least knowingly, to have a president use the Oval Office like a harem or live well on a fortune masterminded by an unscrupulous patriarch (Joseph Kennedy) willing to break every law but those of physics to secure his family's future—that is, his sons' futures in politics.

For those who weren't there—either they hadn't yet been born or they weren't at ground zero of the fervor for civil rights—it's hard to understand how and why the director of the FBI, even given his notorious paranoia, would be so terrified of the movement whose ultimate aim, after all, was full implementation of the Constitution that he'd sworn to protect. Putting as charitable a spin on it as possible, the answer is the Cold War. It was then at its peak—indeed, the Cuban missile crisis that had nearly led to a full-scale nuclear war between the United States and the USSR was only eight months in the past—and Hoover believed, or believed that his job required him to believe, that the Soviets were this close to undermining, if not ending, "our American way of life."

The paranoia that began after Mao came to power in 1949, with everyone asking Harry Truman, not so rhetorically, "Who lost China?" continued through Joe McCarthy, duck-and-cover drills in schools, Ho Chi Minh in Vietnam, the French fleeing Dien Bien Phu, Soviet tanks in Hungary, Sputnik and the space race, the fall of Cuba to Castro, and Castro's embrace of Russia. To certain people paid to be afraid, it did at the time seem entirely plausible, if not possible, that our Jeffersonian republic would fall, toppled not so much by an invasion from some outside enemy as by communist agents inside the United States itself inciting the populace to revolt. There may even have appeared to be a certain inevitability to the revolution, as though Lenin's comment that we'd gladly sell them the rope to hang ourselves had been a prophecy instead of a wisecrack.

To Hoover and a great many other people whose job was to worry about such things, the civil rights movement was a threat to the status quo, and any threat to the status quo was ipso facto a threat to the United States. Everything new could be considered subversive: Elvis, for example— another drop of red dye that would one day accumulate in sufficient quantities to tint the whole country. Their line of reasoning encompassed the Arab aphorism that "the enemy of my enemy is my friend." In other words, civil rights leaders, advocates, and workers would make common cause with communists or become fellow travelers themselves.

I mention this only as a way of providing some generous context for the complete treachery of J. Edgar Hoover and the tepid political courage of John F. Kennedy—a man who feared that any domestic embarrassment would make him look weak to the Soviets, as if in a democracy the right of the people to assemble and petition their government for grievance reflected a leadership vacuum ripe for exploitation. This explains why he tried to talk Martin and the SCLC leadership out of holding the March on Washington later that summer—because it would be better to succeed in Congress than to hold a "big show" at the Capitol.

"I have some bad news for you," JFK told Martin. And the bad news was something his brother the attorney general had told him. "Hoover says that some people close to you are communists."

Martin scoffed at the idea that he'd been "infiltrated."

No, not infiltrated, Kennedy said. "Two of your closest advisers."

Knowing Hoover, Martin half expected to hear that his wife Coretta was one of them. He later told me that he wanted to laugh but didn't. These were serious times with a lot at stake.

"Who?" he asked.

"Stanley Levison and Jack O'Dell."

The news could hardly have been worse and Martin didn't need the president to explain the ramifications, though he let him go on anyway. Armed with this kind of information, Kennedy said, the southern segregationists could derail the civil rights bill he was about to introduce, citing commie infiltration of the Movement. The last thing Kennedy needed was to take a chance politically, only to get shot down on the blind side.

"I don't want to be in Macmillan's position," he said.

Just a few months before, England's defense minister, John Profumo, was caught enjoying himself extramaritally with a showgirl named Christine Keeler. When questioned about it in the House of Commons, Profumo lied and a scandal ensued that led to his resignation.

Even in those more puritanical times, what soon became known as the "Profumo affair" was not, strictly speaking, about sex or adultery. The issue, insofar as the British public and politicians were concerned, was that a man holding such an important position might possibly be sharing pillow-talk state secrets with a beautiful young woman who, as it happened, was also seeing a Russian naval attaché posted to the Soviet embassy in London. The secondary scandal revolved around Prime Minister Harold Macmillan's stalwart defense of his friend and cabinet minister.

Profumo had just resigned when JFK led Martin on that Rose Garden walk, and already it was clear that Macmillan had been fatally compromised—in fact he would resign a few months later.

"Macmillan's going to lose his government because he was too loyal to a friend," the president said.

To Kennedy, the analogy was clear. How ironic, given what we know now about JFK's own proclivities, which included sharing the same mistress as Mafia don Sam Giancana.

Kennedy warned Martin that the civil rights bill couldn't be shepherded through Congress until he knew for sure that there was no danger of Martin being tainted by communist associations, because those would in turn taint the president. Apparently Hoover had already shared his suspicions about Levison and O'Dell with Everett Dirksen, the senior senator from Illinois and the Senate's minority leader—the Republican Kennedy most needed to offset the votes he expected to lose from his own party members in the South (Bull Connor, after all, was a prominent Democrat in Alabama); he wanted Dirksen as a Senate cosponsor of the bill, something Dirksen couldn't manage politically if it "came out" that he'd been cautioned ahead of time about the ongoing connections between the most prominent leader of the Movement and known commies.

Worse, Kennedy suggested, the Movement might lose all the momentum it was gaining from the outrage over Birmingham, and the entire civil rights apparatus could crumble from a loss of white support, both financial and moral.

"You must be careful not to lose your cause for the same reason as Macmillan," Kennedy said. "Get rid of these guys, Levison and O'Dell—and let me know that it's been done."

Martin didn't believe the allegations but promised the president that he'd investigate and report back. What other choice did he have? Saying no and risking everything was not an option.

Stanley Levison was invaluable to Martin personally and, because of that, to the Movement itself. Martin considered Stanley one of his "winter soldiers," and the thought of not working with him again—worse, not speaking to him on a daily basis—twisted Martin's stomach and conscience. As for O'Dell, another confidant, though less important, Martin said he'd hold off doing anything until he determined Stanley's status; he admitted it wouldn't have surprised him to learn that Jack had communist sympathies and contacts, if only for his professed admiration of Paul Robeson and the Soviet Union's reputation as antiracist.

When Martin told me about Kennedy's ultimatum, I jerked my knee, so to speak.

"Oh," I said, "so they don't think Negroes are smart enough to know what's in our own best interests in our own country unless the communists tell us."

Indeed, one of the standard arguments against integration by its most vocal opponents was that our demands for racial justice weren't based on actual injustices but were instead a fiction dreamed up by the commies to embarrass the United States. Negroes, in other words, had been duped and manipulated by the Communist Party USA—under orders, of course, direct from Moscow.

Martin had been mentally there and back already by the time he listened to my rant, but he didn't see the value in cursing the mountain before climbing it. He simply asked, "Do you think Stanley's a member of the party?"

"What do I think?" I said. "What do I think? Martin, you've known him a lot longer than I have. Have you ever discussed it with him?"

"No, I haven't, but I don't believe he is," he said, and I thought that was that. But to my surprise, he added that he was appointing me to "conduct an independent inquiry" and report back to him, so that he himself could report to JFK my "findings and recommendations."

He gave me until the SCLC board met later that month, at a work retreat in Asheville, North Carolina, to complete the job.

I almost laughed. "How do you suggest I conduct an independent inquiry?"

"Meet with Stanley and Jack, but do it separately. Ask them about any association with communist groups, and then check around with people who know them and their friends."

"Martin," I said, "this sounds like a witch hunt—something Joe McCarthy would've done ten years ago."

"No," he said, "it's something the FBI does when you apply for a government job—a background check. Besides, Clarence, the president and the attorney general expect me to conduct a good-faith inquiry, and that's what I intend to do."

I reminded him that appeasing the Kennedy administration was a slippery political slope and reminded him of the words of Martin Niemoller as quoted by Milton Mayer in *They Thought They Were Free*, published in 1955. Mayer writes:

> Pastor Niemoller spoke with thousands . . . and said that, when the Nazis attacked the Communists, he was a little uneasy, but, after all, he was not a Communist, and so he did nothing; and then they attacked the Socialists, and he was a little uneasier, but, still, he was not a Socialist, and he did nothing; and then the schools, the press, the Jews, and so on, and he was always uneasier, but still he did nothing. And then they attacked the Church, and he was a Churchman, and he did something—but then it was too late.

Martin's eyes filled. "Since when," I said, "can the government dictate who's qualified and eligible to work for a civil rights leader?"

"When there's so much riding on it," he said, more annoyed with himself for having to answer than he was with me for challenging him. Martin was a dreamer, yes, but he knew the meaning of Pyrrhic victory. Not all principles were created equal. Some were worth fighting and dying for, and some weren't worth a lost war. That didn't mean he had to like it.

"Believe me, Clarence, I like this less than you do," he said when I told him the assignment made me want to puke.

Stanley and I met. I expressed how embarrassing this was for me. He listened to my rambling preamble intended to put my question into context, then listened to the question itself—and immediately put me at ease with his lack of defensiveness. He had, he admitted, worked with the CP-USA some seven to ten years before, along with his identical twin brother, while both were students at City College of New York. As was the case with Jack O'Dell, the impetus had been civil rights and social justice—both of which were then presumed by large numbers of people, perhaps naïvely, to be part of the Soviet Union's worker's paradise. But then in Stanley's mind, at least, paradise turned to hell after the Soviets' brutal invasion and suppression of Hungary in 1956; it soured him on communism and communists, he said, guaranteeing me that he hadn't had any subsequent connection with the party.

Nonetheless, for the good of the Movement and Martin and American Negroes in general, he volunteered to have no direct contact with Martin for as long as necessary.

"The FBI," he said, "will use any excuse to destroy you. You have to take away all their excuses. You tell Martin to tell the president and the attorney general that he's cut all ties with me. He's got a movement to lead, and it has nothing to do with me and our relationship. We can't be sentimental about it."

In biblical terms, appropriate here, this was akin to the mother of the infant whom King Solomon had ordered cut in half offering to give her child to the other woman in order to stave off the killing. The difference was that J. Edgar Hoover was no Solomon, and Stanley's magnanimous willingness to put the Movement's interests above his own was not rewarded by anything other than the Movement's and Martin's gratitude. It broke Martin's heart, not being able to see Stanley or even talk directly to him; and it also embarrassed him that he essentially had to excommunicate one of his most loyal supporters, advisers, and financial contributors—someone who was neither black nor a clergyman but a Jewish white man.

From then on, any contact between Martin and Stanley would be indirect. I was the conduit. I continued to speak with Stanley often, sometimes every day, though I didn't always pass on his words or advice as Stanley's; Martin, after all, needed plausible deniability—deniability that would soon be undone by wiretaps.

There is a bitterly sardonic P.S. to Stanley's story that I've never managed to forget: After he had left the party to concentrate on his successful businesses—among them a car dealership in New Jersey and coin-operated laundries in Ecuador—Stanley was approached by FBI agents and asked to become an informant. Obviously, they knew he'd left the Communist Party or they wouldn't have pitched him so many years back. But because he had said no, that apparently made him suspect enough for Hoover to tell RFK to tell JFK to tell MLK. That would be breathtaking enough if it weren't for the kicker: the informant who originally fed Stanley's name to the FBI was the husband of Stanley's first wife, who happened to be Harry Belafonte's first manager.

Truth, stranger than fiction.

For his part, Jack O'Dell admitted to a membership in the CP-USA, before joining the SCLC in the 1950s, while he was an organizer for the National Maritime Union. Like Stanley, Jack offered to resign from the SCLC and was hired to run an affiliate voter registration project. Even so, he did not go quietly. Meeting with several of us in Martin's New York City hotel room, he angrily shouted, "You tell Hoover and Kennedy to kiss my black ass." Neither of them, he insisted, was worthy to decide who was acceptable to the movement. Now Martin reported back to JFK that he'd done what was appropriate for the president to go forward in good faith. If only that had ended the story.

2

Robert Kennedy had several strikes against him. For one, he'd been appointed the attorney general of the United States by his brother, a fact that made him defensive about how nepotism had gotten him a job for which he had neither adequate experience nor talent. (Talk about affirmative action.) For another, he'd been born defensive anyway, as well as prickly. Probably more than any of his siblings, he most resembled his father, Joseph P. Kennedy, in terms of taste and temperament—that is, he could be a real son of a bitch, especially in those days, before his brother's assassination.

As much as his brother the president, Robert Kennedy was a political creature who, long before President Clinton made it famous by doing it better than anyone, understood the triangulation of competing interests. For instance his Department of Justice, in 1962, ordered federal troops and U.S. marshals to protect James Meredith as he became the first black student to attend the University of Mississippi, thanks to the Supreme Court's ruling of a year before confirming that he'd previously been denied admission solely on account of his race. And to counter any political repercussions from those inclined to call his actions "nigger loving," Robert Kennedy also oversaw the appointment of several outspoken segregationists to the federal bench.

Even so, on balance, as a man of his time, Robert Kennedy's record on civil rights was to the good, if only because it made political sense—or sometimes because Martin

Luther King, among others, prodded and poked him to do the right thing. For example, at Martin's "suggestion," he convened a grand jury in Macon, Georgia, to investigate and prosecute police and civilian brutality during the failed Albany demonstrations.

In May 1963, aware of grumblings among the black intelligentsia that the Kennedy administration was doing too little and moving too slowly, Robert Kennedy asked the great novelist James Baldwin to organize a quiet, off-the-record, unpublicized get-together of prominent Negroes so that he could plead his case and, he promised, listen to their concerns. The meeting took place one evening at the Central Park West apartment of Kennedy's brother-in-law, Stephen Smith, who, not coincidentally, had recently begun his work as President Kennedy's reelection campaign manager.

Representing the black world were writers Jimmy Baldwin and Lorraine Hansberry, entertainers Lena Horne and Harry Belafonte, educator and psychologist Kenneth Clark, and a bright young black civil rights worker from Mississippi named Jerome Smith. (There was another man, too, the white actor Rip Torn, a friend of Jimmy's who would star the following year on Broadway as a vicious white racist in Jimmy's second play, *Blues for Mr. Charlie*, based on Emmett Till's lynching in 1955 Mississippi for allegedly whistling at a white woman.) I was present as a representative of Martin Luther King, who wasn't there for reasons I no longer remember.

From the beginning of the meeting, it seemed, Robert Kennedy was less eager to listen to the assembly's opinion that race relations, even in the North, had become "explosive" than to extol himself and his brother's administration for moving as quickly as possible on civil rights.

At some point Jerome Smith started weeping, the tears appearing to come out of nowhere, as if he'd just suffered some traumatic flashback. As he rocked in grief and pain, he blurted out that being there in the room with Robert Kennedy made him "want to vomit." He said, "You guys are full of shit," referring to the Justice Department. "I've seen you guys stand around and do nothing more than take notes while we're being beaten."

As you might imagine, Kennedy recoiled, looked at the rest of us for some help, and started to defend himself. But then Lorraine and Lena jumped in. Lena said to him, "You have to hear what's being said to you. We're trying to interpret the pain and fear and apprehension about what's going on."

Lorraine drove in the last nail. "You've got a great many very, very accomplished people in this room, but the only man who should be listened to is that man over there," she said, meaning Jerome.

Kennedy was visibly shaken. It was clear to me that he'd never had any group of people, let alone Negroes, talk to him like that. And the person on whom he vented his anger was me, Martin Luther King's attorney. Apparently he felt that I had an obligation to speak up on his behalf and inform the people in that room about all the wonderful things his Department of Justice had tried to do in Birmingham.

Instead, I'd offered a suggestion that, as writer Taylor Branch noted, Robert Kennedy must've thought reflected my hopeless naïveté about politics—though it couldn't have been any more hopeless than Kennedy's ignorance of race. He had actually laughed aloud when I suggested that he make a grand dramatic gesture against segregation by announcing that he planned to walk hand in hand with

black students into the University of Alabama, and if necessary confront Governor Wallace's state troopers charged
with blocking their way.

Kennedy also scoffed when I suggested, recalling FDR's
fireside chats, that his brother the president ought to prepare a series of short televised speeches on the evils of segregation and discrimination.

I hadn't said anything in favor of the administration because I didn't consider it my job to play the role of Good
Negro, acting as Justice's PR flack. At that moment I remembered JFK's exasperation when the white leaders of Albany, Georgia, refused to meet with Martin and the other
civil rights leaders. He'd said, "We sit down with the Soviets
in Geneva. Why can't we sit down with some of our fellow
citizens here at home?" Clearly, the administration's entire
worldview was through the prism of what made the president look capable and strong to the Russians. As such, Robert Kennedy seemed to think that the people in that room
represented not the great grassroots masses of Negroes in
America, but rather our most militant and extremist ele-
ments—that is to say, the mirror image of white segregationists—and we had to be dealt with accordingly.

In fact, that's precisely the viewpoint that appeared in
journalist James Reston's account in the *New York Times* of
what was supposed to be that off-the-record meeting (until
James Baldwin leaked some details to another reporter and
the Kennedys called in a favor). Reston, of course, was a
friend of and to the Kennedys, so his account may as well
have been ghostwritten by Robert Kennedy himself.

To correct that one-sided report, I wrote a letter to the
Times—and to make certain that Bobby saw it, I cc'ed him
as well. In the letter I noted that though the Kennedy administration had been more vigorous than any previous

administration in prosecuting civil rights violations, its actions were still anything but commensurate with the enormity of both the violations and the crisis at hand, which in essence reflected the view that we Negroes were asking for too much too soon, as Martin had written in his "Letter from a Birmingham Jail."

I wrote, "When the chief legal officer of the United States displays a certain shock over the sentiments expressed . . . that fact in and of itself . . . is indicative of how the Administration underestimates the explosive ingredients inherent in the continued existence of racial discrimination and segregation."

What I didn't include in the letter but, on reflection, perhaps should have, was that it had been Robert Kennedy's brother, the president, who had been prescient enough to note "those who make peaceful change impossible, make violent revolution inevitable."

If Robert Kennedy had become angry before, he was now apoplectic. I brought up with Martin that perhaps I'd become a liability too, the same as Stanley and Jack, and that maybe I ought to step away for the sake of the movement. Martin only laughed.

"I understand you're persona non grata around the Justice Department," he said. "Looks like the Attorney General of the United States regards you as an uppity Negro. But that's all right. We still love you. You're *our* uppity Negro."

3

In July 1963, a month after the president offered his civil rights bill to Congress and a month before the March on Washington, Martin Luther King and his family stayed for two weeks at my home in the Riverdale section of the

Bronx. During that time we fretted over the march, worked on drafts of his "I Have a Dream" speech, and relaxed whenever possible. I also occasionally did some work at the law firm of Lubell, Lubell & Jones, which I'd cofounded with partners Jonathan and David Lubell, who were so understanding of my situation that they frequently carried me during the firm's early years; had they not, my work with Martin would have been either compromised or impossible. Almost every day my wife would call to tell me that the "phone company repairmen are here again, working on our line." By the third day I figured out what was going on and told Anne to put one of them on. "You say hello to Hoover for me," I told him.

Little did I know that J. Edgar Hoover would soon have read a transcript of that hello himself. My phone was indeed being tapped, and prominent historians have suggested that the tap had been authorized by Robert Kennedy out of anger or vengeance for that meeting in New York (following which he'd told his colleagues in Justice that I and other Negro men who'd married white women were suffering from psychological complexes). The official memorandum from Hoover to Kennedy about physically placing the tap references Kennedy's personal "request that in view of the possible communist influence in the racial situation, consideration be given to placing a technical surveillance on Jones."

Not till years later, thanks to the Freedom of Information Act, did I know just how treacherous the FBI and the Department of Justice had been—how relentlessly they'd tried to undermine, if not derail, the civil rights movement. For all of English's hundreds of thousands of words, not one can express the revulsion and outrage one feels when discovering that the director of the Federal Bureau of Investigation overruled his field agents and refused to push the prosecution of the men who blew up the Sixteenth Street Baptist Church in Alabama and murdered those four girls; instead, Hoover accused the civil rights movement itself of the act as a way of inciting action.

Reading through boxes and boxes of verbatim conversations that I'd had in the 1960s was almost as fascinating as it was terrifying. But only almost. My dominant emotion was anger, not least because the wiretaps that began on my home and places of business in the summer of 1963, before the March on Washington, would whet the bureau's appetite and soon lead to taps of Martin wherever he resided or did business.

Now, for the first time, and by sheer dumb luck on the part of the FBI, agents were able to eavesdrop on Martin Luther King. Suffice it to say that, in private, in my home, with me, Martin let down his defenses and relaxed, which meant that for the first time the bureau could hear a side of him it could only have imagined and hoped for, and that must've pleased Hoover's prurience as well as added another chit to his blackmail box—the one that politicians, especially including the Kennedys, lived in fear of.

Worse, though, than the wiretaps in some ways was the discovery that these taps were merely effective supplements to inside information the FBI was already receiving from informants.

Traitors.

Spies.

Years later, when I began reading transcripts of memorable meetings between Martin and me and others, I sometimes noticed that one name was not listed as a participant in the meeting. Clearly, though, I remembered that person being there, which of course led me to deduce who the mole was. In time, I identified two of them, one black and one white (not Stanley, it goes without saying). For obvious reasons, I can't divulge their names without being sued. That doesn't mean I wasn't as surprised and hurt as Martin would've been to learn that not only was his own government out to destroy him, but it was being aided and abetted by people on the inside whom he'd trusted.

The 1976 final report of the Senate's Select Committee charged with investigating domestic surveillance began this way:

"From December 1963 until his death in 1968, Martin Luther King Jr. was the target of an intensive campaign by the Federal Bureau of Investigation to 'neutralize' him as an effective civil rights leader. In the words of the man in charge of the FBI's war against Dr. King: 'No holds were barred. We have used [similar] techniques against Soviet agents. [The same methods were] brought home against any organization against which we were targeted. We did not differentiate. This is a rough, tough business.'"

Of course, it hadn't taken the federal government more than a minute or so after World War II to recognize that America's main enemy in the world was now the Soviet Union. But this was 1963, and it took the FBI until the day after Martin delivered his "I Have a Dream" speech—seven years after Montgomery—to decide, in the then classified words of Agent W. C. Sullivan, that Martin's "powerful demagogic speech yesterday" stands him "head and shoulders over all other Negro leaders put together when it comes to influencing great masses of Negroes. We must mark him now, if we have not done so before, as the most dangerous Negro of the future in this nation from the standpoint of communism, the Negro, and national security."

The long Senate report explains in extraordinary detail how the hidden surveillance of America's "most dangerous

Negro" and the other efforts to destroy him not only continued but intensified after JFK's assassination and RFK's
resignation as attorney general. No resources were spared
or imagination restrained, probably because of Hoover's
own animus—or, in the words of the report, "extreme personal vindictiveness." The bureau found ways to "discredit
him with churches, universities, and the press" and under-
cut his "reception by foreign heads of state and American
ambassadors in the countries that he planned to visit" after
winning the Nobel Peace Prize in 1964. "When the FBI
learned that Dr. King intended to visit the Pope, an agent
was dispatched to persuade Francis Cardinal Spellman to
warn the Pope about 'the likely embarrassment that may
result to the Pope should he grant King an audience.'" The
pope, however, had already met with Martin the previous
September.

It's now well-known that the FBI unilaterally expanded
its authority by hiding microphones in Martin's hotel
rooms, hoping to catch him in recorded behavior that could
be used, Hoover must've hoped, to discredit him as leader
of the Movement. Indeed, the bureau sent a copy of one
tape to Martin along with a note that indicated it would
be made public unless Martin—what follows is not a mis-
print—committed suicide.

"You know you are a complete fraud and a great liability to all of us Negroes," the note said in part. "White
people in this country have enough frauds of their own but
I am sure they don't have one at this time that is anywhere
near your equal. You are no clergyman and you know it.
I repeat you are a colossal fraud, and an evil vicious one
at that. . . . King, like all frauds your end is approaching.
You could have been our greatest leader. . . . But you are
done. Your 'honorary' degrees, your Nobel Prize (what

a grim farce) and other awards will not save you. King, I repeat you are done. . . . King, there is only one thing left for you to do. You know what it is. You have just 34 days in which to do (this exact number has been selected for a specific reason). . . . You are done. There is but one way out for you."

The FBI must've thought it was a clever touch, sending the note from "us Negroes." The image of a bunch of smug frat boys sitting around laughing as they composed this letter is belied by its truly evil intent.

Discrediting Martin and undermining him became far more important, and urgent, when Martin gave voice to the concerns that he'd been sharing with all of us in private, and publicly declared his opposition to the Vietnam War.

On April 4, 1967, exactly one year to the day before his assassination, speaking at Riverside Church in New York, he called the United States "the greatest purveyor of violence in the world." He said that if the United States continues the war, "there will be no doubt in my mind and in the mind of the world that we have no honorable intentions in Vietnam . . . that our minimal expectation is to occupy it as an American colony and men will not refrain from thinking that our maximum hope is to goad China into a war so that we may bomb her nuclear installations."

These were provocative words, born of his having seen riots in American cities each of the previous few summers and fully expecting more violence elsewhere in the coming summers—if not winters, falls, and springs. To the powers that be, though, Martin's words were confirmation of his danger to America. In their eyes, he'd made common cause with the enemy—Red China—accusing his own country of waging war deliberately as a pretext for doing something that, to them, he should've applauded. When he did that, Martin transformed himself, in their eyes, into an enemy of the state. What they missed was that he wanted to avoid violence in the streets at least as much as they did.

4

Again, it's hard now to imagine how terrified Hoover and his bureau, right down to every agent on the street, were in 1968 about the possibility of revolution in this country. Martin, of course, was unaware that the domestic intelligence apparatus had made him a locus of their fears. But it would be unworthy of him for me not to try to put their fears into historical context. The man who said, "You can bomb our houses and our churches, and we will still love you. You can take us out to some dirt road, on a dark night, beat and lynch us, we will still love you. . . . Our power of redemptive love will triumph over your violence and misguided attachment to white supremacy"—the extraordinary man who said that, and meant it, would want me to offer the other "side," such as it was. And that I can do because I've met FBI agents from that era and have heard stories that surprised even me. I'm not defending anything I'm about to pass on. I'm merely reporting, as Martin would want me to.

To understand the FBI's fears, if not paranoia, forget everything you know, or think you know or remember, about the 1960s. Forget about flower power and hippies and LSD and free love; about nonviolent war protests and idealism and civil rights marches; about never trusting anyone over 30 and the Beatles singing "All You Need Is Love" and half a million kids rolling in the mud at Woodstock. Forget JFK, LBJ, Nixon—and even, for a moment, Martin Luther King.

Instead, think for a moment about H. Bruce Franklin. You probably don't recognize the name, which the FBI considers absolute proof that it did its job—because if it hadn't, goes the logic, no one now would recall that decade fondly as an era of love and peace, high hopes, idealism, and brotherliness.

So who was H. Bruce Franklin? Franklin graduated from Amherst in 1955 and served four years with distinction in the U.S. Air Force. In 1961, he received his Ph.D. from Stanford, became an assistant professor of English there, spent a year lecturing at Johns Hopkins, and returned to Palo Alto a tenured professor with a national reputation as an expert on the works of Herman Melville. So far, so good; by age 31, the man had distinguished himself and, with job security at one of the country's elite universities, he could look forward to decades of writing, reading, teaching, quiet contemplation, paid sabbaticals, and guest chairs at other elite universities—the perfect life imagined by any aspiring academic who'd grown up in the 1940s and '50s.

Then came the fall of 1966, which by my reckoning was the third year of turmoil begun by JFK's assassination, now kicked into overdrive by the body bags coming home from Vietnam and our cities going up in flames at the hands of angry blacks whose rage made them deaf to Martin's pleas. Franklin was sent for a semester to Stanford's French campus, near Paris, where he and his wife Jane read a shelf full of Marxist texts after hooking up with some proselytizing Vietnamese communists. Overnight, both Franklins were turned into committed Marxist-Leninists—revolutionaries who denounced America, capitalism, and American "imperialism." Like Perry Como improbably becoming Kanye West, this tweed-clad English prof had somehow morphed into Che Guevara.

On his return home, Franklin wrote a series of articles under the pseudonym "Will B. Outlaw" for a journal called *Maverick*, a publication of the Bay Area Revolutionary Union, which was a collective of groups that espoused violent overthrow of the government and, to that end, urged its members to carry firearms. Mixing polemics with weapons advice, the articles predicted, and warned against, passage of gun-control laws that would make it harder for revolutionaries to kill "pigs" and soldiers.

"We no longer have the right to bear arms," he wrote, "but we can still keep them in our home. So this might be a good time to start thinking about the day when only us outlaws—and the cops—will have guns. Now's the time to figure out what kind of gun we want to have then, because we're going to have to get them pretty quick." And: "In a police state, one necessary tool is a good, reliable pocket pistol. After long looking around and lots of testing, I'm personally convinced that there's one gun in this class that stands out."

When even the RU stopped being revolutionary enough for Franklin, he cofounded the Venceremos ("we shall overcome") Brigade, a largely Chicano group that adopted Maoism for its goal of "national liberation and international revolution."

But in time Venceremos dumped him, and then so did Stanford—and eventually the Venceremos and the RU and the rest of the radical leftist groups, including the Weather Underground, were either defeated or coopted or dissolved. Some of them imploded, and anyone who prefers liberty to tyranny should celebrate that. Believe me. All those guys running around with bandanas shouting "Revolution!" and "Power to the people!" hadn't the least idea what to do if indeed that revolution had come to pass. My sense, though, is that we might've seen wholesale murder to make the killing fields of Cambodia look tame.

Anyway, the point isn't specifically H. Bruce Franklin and what became of him (though you'll be interested to hear that he's now "Howard B. Franklin," the John Cotton Dana Professor of English and American Studies at Rutgers, where his official bio had only this to say about his rabble-rousing past: "Franklin has published continually on the history and literature of the Vietnam War since 1966, when he became widely known for his activist opposition to the war"). No, what makes Franklin important is only what he symbolized at the time, because it's exactly what terrified people in law enforcement: if a straight arrow like this guy could change so completely and become so radicalized, then anyone could—meaning, the hundreds of thousands, if not millions, of kids, most of them white and in college, many from "good" homes and the beneficiaries of trust funds.

In the words of a rock song by a group called Thunderclap Newman, there really was "something in the air." If you were young and white and didn't know better—and if you were young and white you probably didn't—you saw pretty girls with long hair and painted faces flashing peace signs and dropping daisies down the barrels of National Guardsmen's rifles. You saw protest marches organized by romantics and idealists whose only aim was to stop the war. You saw Ed Sullivan shaking hands with psychedelic rock bands, and the Smothers Brothers winking at inside drug jokes. And it was all fun and games, and antiwar rallies were great aphrodisiacs.

What you didn't see was what FBI agents saw below the surface—protest leaders like Tom Hayden and Peter Clapp traveling to Hanoi, Moscow, and Peking; transcripts of decrypted Venona cables that offered proof of Soviet spy networks in the United States; bank accounts funded from overseas being used to buy weapons, ammunition, and matériel; millions of people in the streets, sniffing that same heady something in the air, ripe for one talented demagogue to come along and say the magic words that could've nudged the tipping point and turn them into a revolutionary mob. Don't laugh. As far as the FBI was concerned, it had happened in Russia in 1917. It had happened in Italy in 1922. It had happened in Germany in 1933. It had happened in China in 1949. And it could've happened here—with that talented demagogue being, among others, Martin Luther King.

Remember, according to the FBI, his "powerful demagogic speech" calling for brotherhood had stood him "head and shoulders over all other Negro leaders put together when it comes to influencing great masses of Negroes."

But by 1968, it wasn't just "masses of Negroes" anymore. The moment Martin in essence expanded his moral cause by coming out against the Vietnam War—which was, let's face it, the issue closest to the hearts of those millions of white kids who didn't want to get their asses shot off—he became the five-star general of a much larger army. And as far as J. Edgar Hoover and everyone in charge of maintaining the status quo was concerned, that magnified his danger. After all, if you were convinced that he was a commie or took his orders directly or indirectly from Moscow or Peking or Havana, you were scared witless every time he opened his mouth. Not since Hitler had a man come along with such a gift for oratory.

"I'm not a consensus leader," Martin said when whites pounded him for his opposition to the war. "I don't determine what is right or wrong by looking at the budget of the

Southern Christian Leadership Conference, . . . by roaming around taking a Gallup poll of the majority opinion. . . . There comes a time when one must take a stand that is neither expedient, that's neither safe, that's neither politic, or that is neither popular. But he must take that stand because it is right, and that is where I find myself today."

The crowds cheered, and the feds hunkered down. How they could have mistaken Martin for a violent revolutionary is a mystery no imagination can fathom.

"The anger of many Negroes," Martin declared in 1966 when true radicals like Stokely Carmichael were advocating violent revolution, "has driven them to passive cynicism toward society; for others it has exploded in violence. . . . The only just and moral response from the larger society is that the conditions were created by men and can be removed by men."

For these men, seeing Martin Luther King dead was preferable to removing the conditions that kept others from loving their own country.

5

I don't just believe, I know for certain that James Earl Ray pulled the trigger on the rifle that fired the bullet that killed Martin Luther King. But did he act alone, without accomplices or help? If so, it would be the first time since slavery that a white man driven by racial animus acted by himself to murder a black man. The Klan's anonymity was guaranteed both by their hoods and by their numbers. And lynch mobs were, well, mobs made up of people who would never have had the courage or the strength to act alone. "The willingness of lynchers to act publicly is tremendously significant. It reflects the lynchers' certainty that they would never face punishment for their acts," author Sherrilyn Ifill wrote in *On the Courthouse Lawn: Confronting the Legacy of Lynching in the Twenty-first Century*. "The willingness of the crowd to participate in lynching—to cheer, to yell their encouragement, or just to stand and watch without intervention—is perhaps equally terrible." Even the swine who tortured and killed defenseless 14-year-old Emmett Till didn't act alone. Neither had the man who planted the bomb that blew up the Sixteenth Street Baptist Church and killed the four Sunday School girls. Et cetera, et cetera, et cetera—too many et ceteras to count.

Of course, like the coward he was, Ray protested his innocence until the end of his life, which tells me that he was more afraid of the people he was protecting than he was of facing the devil himself. That says something.

It's impossible not to point a finger at the FBI. Not just because of the mysterious phone call that got Martin to move from a hotel in a white part of Memphis to the black-owned Lorraine Motel, whose rooms could be accessed only by walking up exterior stairs and along an outside walkway, nor because Martin's room number, 306, had been leaked by someone to the press a day ahead of time. No, I point a finger at the FBI because, as the Senate Committee's report acknowledged, the bureau seemed to know everything about Martin Luther King. That agents weren't aware of a plot against him seems about as likely as the Loch Ness Monster's existence. That the agents did nothing to stop the plot, or even warn him, is as unconscionable as doing nothing to prevent the murder of *any* innocent, let alone someone as important as Martin. But of course, there had been other plots against him that either we—those in the Movement—or the local police uncovered or averted ahead of time. For instance, after Malcolm X's murder in February 1965, we learned that white segregationists planned to shoot Martin in Selma, where he'd been four days earlier when Jimmie Lee Jackson was shot.

Jimmie was 26 years old, a farm laborer and church deacon who'd been marching for voting rights to the Perry County Courthouse in Selma when state troopers attacked the crowd with billy clubs. Seeing his mother and grandfather assaulted, he'd run to their aid and was shot in the stomach by an Alabama state trooper (who wouldn't be arrested and charged until 2007). The shot didn't kill him, though, at least not right away. As he lay suffering (anyone who knows anything about stomach wounds understands suffering; imagine the worst stomachache you've ever had times 50), troopers had actually dragged him away so he could be arrested and charged with assault and battery. Not till much later did he reach the hospital.

It took him nine days to die—and nine days after he did, the SCLC and Martin led the first voting rights march from Selma to Montgomery, attracting thousands of volunteers from all over who'd been outraged by the clubs, whips, chains, tear gas, and bullets they saw on the news being used against their defenseless—and undefended—fellow humans. Just as Martin had predicted, their consciences activated and shamed them to moral action.

One of the volunteers, a white Unitarian minister and father of four from Washington, D.C., named James Reeb, was savagely beaten to death by a mob of angry whites armed with clubs. Soon after we put him to rest, a 40-year-old white mother of five named Viola Liuzzo drove down from Michigan in order to lend support and was shot dead by several Klansmen—one of whom was an FBI informant.

Martin spoke at both funerals, each church packed with

thousands both inside and outside. At Rev. Reeb's funeral, he asked, "Who killed James Reeb? The answer is simple and rather limited when we think of the who. He was murdered by a few sick, demented, and misguided men who have the notion that you express dissent through murder. There is another haunting, poignant, desperate question we are forced to ask this afternoon, a question I asked a few days ago as we funeralized James Jackson. It is the question, *what* killed James Reeb? When we move from the who to the what, the blame is wide and the responsibility grows." It grows, he said, to encompass everyone who stands silent in the face of evil.

I had sent telegrams to the president, the attorney general, and the FBI requesting immediate and comprehensive protection for Martin, though by then I knew to doubt whether the government had any sincere and genuine interest in seeing him kept from harm. Sure enough, my instinct was confirmed years later by internal FBI documents, dated a week after Malcolm's death and while Jimmie lay dying, in which Hoover himself had instructed the bureau not to offer or furnish protection to Martin—"nor is anyone else to be furnished protection."

Apparently, the U.S. Department of *Justice* had no legal obligation to do so. As for the moral obligation—well, that seems hardly debatable. Which makes the assassination of Martin Luther King that much harder to bear, even forty years later.

6

In a world judged by God—which was the world Martin believed we inhabit—it's impossible to imagine that Martin Luther King and James Earl Ray would ever find themselves sharing the same afterlife address. But if, by chance, they happened to one day, these are the words I could easily imagine Martin saying to his assassin:

"Brother Ray, there's no doubt that you shot me dead. With that bullet you changed history in ways only God Almighty understands. But what *I* understand, and what my *family* understands every day, is the amount of nearly unbearable pain you inflicted personally on people who never met you, wouldn't recognize you, and would never have known your name if not for the evil you committed.

"But, as I said so many, many times when I still walked the earth, although I hate what you did, I cannot and do not hate you personally. True, I don't like you in the least; like is one of those emotions that requires respect and decency—and it has to be earned. But in the sense that Christ himself commanded his children to love each other, I still love you and those of your ilk who believed that you were doing God's work by killing me and Jimmie Lee Jackson and Viola Liuzzo and James Reeb and James Chaney and Andrew Goodman and Michael Schwerner and those little girls in the Sixteenth Street Baptist Church—and so many others whose names are lost to the ages. You were not, as you've since discovered, doing God's work. I even forgive you, knowing that you were an ignorant pawn in a larger game you didn't know you were playing till it was too late. Whatever you read or heard or learned that made you think that God wouldn't want all of his children to live together in peace and freedom—well, you were carefully taught, as the song goes, by people whom you no doubt see on a daily basis. I'm sure if you had it to do all over again, knowing what you know now, you'd seek out a better breed of teacher—for instance, Hallie Quinn Brown (feel free to Google her on your dial-up connection down there).

"What disappoints me, Brother Ray, is that even as you lay dying, you never mustered the courage to tell my family and the police and the FBI the who, what, and how of the assassination you couldn't possibly have carried off alone. Perhaps if you had, and asked for forgiveness when it would've meant something, you'd be doing God's work in heaven as I did on earth. What a pity. Secrets taken to the grave weigh you down forever—down, down, down.

"Listen, Brother Ray, you tell J. Edgar Hoover when you see him later that, for all the good things he may have done in his role as chief of the bureau, he unfortunately forgot where in the hierarchy of the universe he stood. God has indeed blessed America, it's true, but a blessing is not a license to disobey His law. Morality always stands above legality, and those who forget that do so at the risk of their souls.

"If you wish, you can cite two quotations I used often during the struggle to free men's consciences. 'No lie can live forever,' Thomas Carlyle said. And, in the words of William Cullen Bryant, 'Truth crushed to earth will rise again.' And then you can follow up with this poem from James Russell Lowell:

> Truth forever on the scaffold, Wrong forever on
>   the throne—
> Yet that scaffold sways the future, and, behind the
>   dim unknown,
> Standeth God within the shadow, keeping watch
>   above his own.

"Amen, Brother. But of course, you and Hoover already know that now. You know that whether it takes another forty years, or a hundred, the truth you've tried to hide about what happened to me and our nation on April 4, 1968, will see the sunlight. And I pray that you do too, someday."

ACKNOWLEDGMENTS

NO BOOK IS CREATED BY ONE PERSON; NOR IS ANY life lived alone. There have been many people who have participated in the journey of my life, and their contributions to the events in which I was involved with Martin and to this book must be noted.

Thank-yous go first and foremost to Joan and Sandy Weill, for their generous support of the Martin Luther King, Jr., Research and Education Institute at Stanford; to Steve Baum, managing partner, Marks Paneth & Shron LLP, without whose support and encouragement this book would not have been written; to all the partners and personnel at Marks Paneth; and to Richard Kronthal and his family for their encouragement. I thank Lin Walters, whose early devotion and dedication of time were inspirational, especially in the organization of voluminous formerly secret and top secret FBI files of transcribed wiretapped conversations with Dr. King that were essential to my ability to accurately reconstruct recollections about several important issues and events described in the book. Thanks go to my friends and supporters at Citigroup—Charles "Chuck" Prince, Raymond J. McGuire, Michael Schlein, Wendy Takahisa, Mike Sharp, Evan Charkes, and A. Mark Mason of Global Wealth Management; and special thanks to Ana McCarthy Duarte, Leah Johnson, and Andrea Mason, whom I affectionately refer to as "the Citi Pretty Women." I thank Craig Menin, "my other son," for his devotion and support; and my friends in Chicago—Abe Thompson, Louis Meyers Esq., Bennett and Cathy Johnson, B. J. and Lisa Johnson. I thank James Mitchell Jr. at General Electric and my friends at British Petroleum for their encouragement. Thanks also go to Mariel Clemensen, John H. Lee, Stephen Rosenberg and the Murray Rosenberg Foundation, and Bonnie Dublin, who were early supporters of my effort to write this book; to Carl E. Dickerson, "the brother I never had," and his wife, Jean, whose consistent love, support, and encouragement over the years have been a special source of inspiration. Thanks go to Ray Negron, Anthony Epps, John Edmonds Esq., the Honorable Percy Sutton, Lainie Cooke, Jamal Joseph, Voza Rivers, Marsha Owens, Chas Walker, Chester and Gladys Redhead, Clem and Doug Pugh, Sonya White of Developing Dreams, Bin Sulaiman, Agieb Bilal, Mal Woolfolk Jr., my former law partners David and Jonathan Lubell, my good friend Ambassador William vanden Heuvel; friends from my Wall Street days, Roger Berlind, Arthur Carter, Arthur Levitt Jr., and Stephen Swid; Rodney and Lisa Fund, Steve Troy, Isaiah Washington, Tavis Smiley, Dr. Cornel West, George Tobia, Doug Brinkley and *Vanity Fair*; Tom Hopke, Cal Morgan, Jonathan Burnham, and Nina Olmsted of HarperCollins; Gerald and Joyce Johnson-Miller, Earnest Flowers III and the Winter Soldiers Group; Mersh and Bonnie Greenberg, Bruce Green, Drs. Sandra Steinman, Jay I. Meltzer, Howard Scher and Zvi Fuks and medical personnel at Memorial Sloan Kettering Cancer Center; Dr. Halstead Holman,

Brenda Schneider and Comerica Bank; the Schomburg Center for Research in Black Culture; Byron Lewis, and Marcia Lyons Wilson. Thanks to my deceased friends and colleagues at Inner City Broadcasting, Sylvia Scholtz and Dr. Mal Woolfolk.

I "thank" the FBI for its meticulous recording of history, which enabled me to have an accurate recollection about events that happened so long ago.

Also, thanks go to my good friends Margo Davis and Anthony Browne, who were responsible for recommending me to be a Scholar in Residence at the King Institute at Stanford.

Special thanks go to Professor Clayborne Carson, director of the Martin Luther King, Jr., Research and Education Institute at Stanford University; to the student research assistants Ryan Peters and Mondaire Jones; and to all the people and staff at the Institute whose assistance and support for my work on this book were magnificent, including Administrator Jane Abbott, Associate Directors Tenisha Armstrong and Susan Englander, Consulting Editor Susan Carson, Research Assistants Madolyn Orr and Louis Jackson, Assistant Director of the Liberation Curriculum Ashni Mohnot, and Assistant Director of Public Programs Regina Covington.

To those heroes who constituted that great moral army of winter soldiers who stood with, worked with, and supported Martin, in good times and bad, I give thanks for all the work and support of the cause: Harry Belafonte; Ruby Dee and Ossie Davis; the Reverends Samuel "Billy" Kyles, James Laws, Gardner Taylor, Wyatt Tee Walker, Sandy Ray, William "Bill" Jones, James Bevel, Jesse Jackson, Fred Shuttelsworth, Joseph Lowery, C. K. Steele, C. T. Vivian, Bernard Lee, and John Lewis; and Jack O'Dell, Dorothy Cotton, Edwina Smith, Dora McDonald, Diane Nash Bevel, Dr. W. G Anderson, C. B. King Esq., Constance Baker Motley, and Jack Greenberg of the NAACP "Inc Fund"; Julian Bond; Moe Foner of Local 1199, Drug, Hospital, and Health Care Employees Union; Leon Davis of the United Retail, Wholesale, and Department Store Union; Ralph Helstein of the United Packinghouse Workers of America in Chicago; Walter Reuther of the United Auto Workers; Joseph Rauh; Unita Blackwell; the Freedom Riders; and others too numerous to name individually here.

I would be remiss if I did not name those who died in the struggle or thereafter or lost their lives in support of Martin's efforts to make the United States live up to its promise and precepts in our Declaration of Independence and Constitution: Ralph Abernathy; Chauncey Eskridge; Anne Aston Warder Norton Jones; Ella Baker; Jimmy Lee Jackson; Viola Liuzzo; Reverend James Reeb; Fannie Lou Hamer and Victoria Gray; Hosea Williams; James Chaney, Michael Schwerner, and Andrew Goodman; Jonathan Daniels; Reverend Thomas Kilgore; Medgar Evers; Herbert Jackson; Rabbi Abraham Heschel; 11-year-old Denise McNair and 14-year-olds Addie Mae Collins, Carole Robertson, and Cynthia Wesley—and those thousands of people, black, white, red, yellow, and brown, Jews, Catholics, Protestants, and others who joined Martin at the March on Washington; who marched with him in Albany, Georgia; in St. Augustine, Florida; in Montgomery, Birmingham, and Selma, Alabama; in Chicago and Cicero, Illinois; in Los Angeles, Cleveland, Boston, Philadelphia, New York City, Atlanta, San Francisco, Memphis, and many other places across America.

To the authors of the Pulitzer Prize–winning accounts

of our struggles, Taylor Branch and David Garrow, I say thank you.

To my deceased friends Lorraine Hansberry, Bobby Nemiroff, Martin "Mickey" Horowitz, and my ex-marine ("Kill them all, let God sort them out," referring to the war in Iraq), politically right wing friend Jonathan H. Edelstein Esq., who loved me and my daughter Felicia with all his heart and soul.

A special additional mention has to be made of Harry Belafonte. Harry, consistently devoted to Martin, was like a beacon of light among performing artists, black and white, summoning them to join with him in support of Martin. He did this at the top of his game, investing his superstar persona and his money in support of Martin, Coretta, and their children.

I certainly owe a debt of gratitude to Mary Elizabeth Toliver Jones and Goldsboro Benjamin Jones, domestic servants and my parents; to the nuns of the Order of the Sacred Heart at Cornwell Heights boarding school; to my science and English teachers and the principal at Palmyra High School, who enabled and facilitated my admission and attendance at Columbia University; and to my children, Christine Jones-Tucker, Alexia Norton Jones, Clarence Benjamin Jones Jr., Dana Nicholas Goldsboro Jones, and Felicia Elizabeth Jones. I hope that, after reading this book, they and their contemporaries, beneficiaries of the legacy of Martin, will better understand the magnitude of his contribution to their lives.

To Joel Engel, an incredibly talented wordsmith with political and artistic integrity, who enabled me to translate my thoughts and words about Martin into a form and style that would engage the reader.

To my editor Doug Grad at HarperCollins: I have come

to understand that all editors take a chance with an unknown author, especially someone who has never written a book before. It was because of his understanding of the importance of the legacy of Martin King that Doug was willing to take that chance on me. I will remain eternally grateful for his assistance, wisdom, and editorial integrity.

SOURCE NOTES

INTRODUCTION

xiii "Congress shall make": *The Constitution of the United States*, Amendment 1.

xiii "A well regulated": *The Constitution of the United States*, Amendment 2.

xv *Plessy v. Ferguson*, 163 U.S. 537 (1896).

xvi "A nation": Martin Luther King, Jr., "The Strength to Love," in James M. Washington, ed., *A Testament of Hope: The Essential Writings and Speeches of Martin Luther King, Jr.* (San Francisco: HarperCollins, 1991), 494.

ONE: WHAT DID MARTIN SAY ABOUT ME?

15 Langston Hughes, *Vintage Hughes* (New York: Vintage Books, 2004), 7–8.

21 *New York Times Co. v. Sullivan*, 376 U.S. 254 (1964).

24 *Sullivan*, 1.

26 Thomas Paine, *Common Sense, The Rights of Man, and Other Essential Writings of Thomas Paine* (New York: Meridian, 1969), 75.

TWO: WHAT WOULD MARTIN SAY ABOUT TODAY'S BLACK LEADERSHIP?

29   Richard Nixon, as quoted in Otto Friedrich, "I Have Never Been a Quitter," *Time*, May 2, 1994.

32   Hillary Clinton, as quoted in Mary Snow and Candy Crowley, "Clinton's 'plantation' remark draws fire," *CNN.com*, January 18, 2006.

33   Joseph Welch, as quoted in Paul Krugman, "At Long Last?" *New York Times*, April 5, 2002.

34   "Life's Most": Martin Luther King, Jr., "Facing the Challenge of a New Age," in Clayborne Carson, Stewart Burns, Susan Carson, Dana Powell, and Peter Holloran, eds., *Birth of a New Age*, Vol. 3, *The Papers of Martin Luther King, Jr.* (Berkeley: University of California Press, 1997), 461.

42   Martin Luther King, Jr., "Address to First Montgomery Improvement Association Mass Meeting, at Holt Street Baptist Church," in Clayborne Carson, ed., *A Call to Conscience: The Landmark Speeches of Martin Luther King, Jr.* (New York: IPM/Warner Books, 2001), 9–10.

42   "My call": Martin Luther King, Jr., as quoted in Lewis V. Baldwin, *There Is a Balm in Gilead: The Cultural Roots of Martin Luther King, Jr.*, (Minneapolis: Fortress Press, 1991), 280.

44   "Nonviolence": Martin Luther King, Jr., "Nobel Prize Acceptance Speech," in James M. Washington, ed., *A Testament of Hope: The Essential Writings and Speeches of Martin Luther King, Jr.* (San Francisco: HarperCollins, 1991), 224.

44   "de Lawd": "Time Person of the Year: Martin Luther King, Jr.," *Time*, January 3, 1964.

45   "the first Negro": James Baldwin, *The Price of the Ticket: Collected Nonfiction, 1948–1985* (New York: St. Martin's Press, 1985), 246.

45   "The power": Baldwin, 262.

46   "God gave us": Martin Luther King, Jr., "Facing the Challenge of a New Age," in Washington, ed., *A Testament of Hope*, 143.

46 "Jena Six": Richard G. Jones, "In Louisiana, a Tree, a Fight, and a Question of Justice," *New York Times*, September 19, 2007.

48 Stefanie Brown, as quoted in Mary Foster, "'Jena Six' rally puts justice system on trial," *The Seattle Times*, September 21, 2007.

48 "There's always": Jones, "In Louisiana, a Tree."

48 "Free the Jena Six": Scott Farwell, "United, they march," *The Dallas Morning News*, September 21, 2007.

49 Lewis V. Baldwin, *Toward the Beloved Community* (Cleveland, Ohio: The Pilgrim Press, 1995), 3.

50 "drop all charges": Maria Moy, "Students show Jena 6 support," *The Flat Hat*, September 21, 2007.

51 "Men and women": Martin Luther King, Jr., "Love, Law, and Civil Disobedience," in Washington, ed., *A Testament of Hope*, 48.

51 "It's wrong": Martin Luther King, Jr., as quoted in "Introduction," in Clayborne Carson, Ralph Luker, Penny A. Russell, and Peter Holloran, eds., *Rediscovering Precious Values, September 1951–November 1955*, Vol. 2, *The Papers of Martin Luther King, Jr.* (Berkeley: University of California Press, 1994), 8.

51 Ernest Hemingway, *By-line: Ernest Hemingway,* William White, ed. (New York: Charles Scribner's Sons, 1967), 27.

51 Martin Luther King, Jr., "Letter from a Birmingham Jail," in Washington, ed., *A Testament of Hope*, 294.

53 "I believe": Martin Luther King, Jr., "Desegregation at Last," in Clayborne Carson, ed., *The Autobiography of Martin Luther King, Jr.* (New York: Warner Books, 1998), 97.

53 "the only": Martin Luther King, Jr., "Rediscovering Lost Values," in Clayborne Carson and Peter Holloran, eds., *A Knock at Midnight: Inspiration from the Great Sermons of Reverend Martin Luther King, Jr.* (New York: Warner Books, 1998), 12–13.

55 "Black women": Reverend Jesse Jackson, Sr., "Duke: Horror and Truth," *Chicago Defender*, April 24, 2006.

55 Ibid.

58   "the nation's oldest": Anita Hamilton and Peter Bailey, "Recharging the Mission," *Time*, January 10, 2005.

59   "I take": Tennie Pierce, as quoted in Christine Pelisek, "What Really Happened at Fire Station 5?" *L.A. Weekly*, March 14, 2007.

60   "Feed the big dog": Tennie Pierce, as quoted in Christine Pelisek, "Tennie Pierce Gets 1.43 Million," *L.A. Weekly*, September 21, 2007.

60   "could potentially": William J. Barber, as quoted in Michael Gaynor, "Duke case: Too much for NC NAACP," *Renew America.us*, January 21, 2007 (http://www.renewamerica. us/columns/gaynor/070121).

61   "classism": William J. Barber, as quoted in Renee Chou, "NAACP Reinforces Call for Law to Resolve Duke Lacrosse Case," *WRAL.com*, December 23, 2006 (http://www.wral .com/news/local/story/1116684/)

61   "The slogan": Martin Luther, King, Jr., "It Is Not Enough to Condemn Black Power," *The New York Times*, July 26, 1966.

62   "there are more black men": Kim Landers, "Jena 6 case sparks anti-racism protest," ABC News.com, September 21, 2007.

62   "pretty soon": John Edwards, as quoted in Terence Samuel, "Where's the plan to get young black men out of jail? In the race," *Chicago Sun-Times*, October 14, 2007.

64   "we still are": DeNeen L. Brown, "A Filmmaker's Attempt to Peel Off the Labels," *Washington Post*, August 4, 2007.

66   "black-on-black": Donovan McNabb, as quoted in Michael Smith, "McNabb: T.O. situation was about money, power," ESPN.com, February 2, 2006 (http://sports.espn.go.com/ nfl/news/story?id=2315565).

THREE: WHAT WOULD MARTIN SAY
ABOUT AFFIRMATIVE ACTION?

70   "arsenal of democracy": U.S. Department of State, "Radio Address Delivered by President Roosevelt From Washington,

December 29, 1940," *Peace and War: United States Foreign Policy, 1931–1941* (Washington, D.C.: U.S., Government Printing Office, 1943).

70   "to take": U.S. Department of Labor, Employment Standards Administration, Office of Federal Contract Compliance Programs, *Facts on Executive Order 11246—Affirmative Action.*

70   President Lyndon B. Johnson, "Commencement Address at Howard University: 'To Fulfill These Rights,'" Washington, D.C.: June 4, 1965.

71   Martin Luther King, Jr., "I Have a Dream," in James M. Washington, ed., *A Testament of Hope: The Essential Writings and Speeches of Martin Luther King, Jr.* (San Francisco: HarperCollins, 1991), 217.

72   Playboy, as quoted in "*Playboy* Interview: Martin Luther King, Jr.," ibid., 367.

72–73   "fair-minded," "compensating": Martin Luther King, Jr., as quoted ibid.

73   "Few people": Martin Luther King, Jr., *Why We Can't Wait* (USA: Penguin, 2000).

74   "freedom": Ibid.

75   "Bill of Rights": Ibid., 127.

75   "a large stratum": Martin Luther King, Jr., "The Other America," Stanford University: April 14, 1967.

75   "I do not intend": Martin Luther King, Jr., *Why We Can't Wait.*

76   "on the outskirts": Ibid.

77   "justice": Martin Luther King, Jr., "Where Do We Go from Here?" in Washington, ed., *A Testament of Hope.*

77   "goals and timetables": Departments of Justice and Labor, Equal Employment Opportunity Commission, and Civil Service Commission, "State and Local Employment Practices Guide," March 23, 1973.

78   Martin Luther King, Jr., "I Have a Dream," in Washington, ed., *A Testament of Hope.*

83   Stanley Crouch, "MTV, Still Clueless After All These Years," *New York Daily News*, August 7, 2006.

85   "segregation": George Wallace, as quoted in Bill Rice, Sr., "History's verdict on George Wallace influenced by passage of time," *The Montgomery Independent*, November 12, 2007.

85   "a few": George Wallace, as quoted in Stephan Lesher, *George Wallace: American Populist* (Reading, MA: Addison-Wesley, 1994).

85   "most dastardly": Martin Luther King, Jr., "Eulogy for the Martyred Children," in Washington, ed., *A Testament of Hope*.

86   "the martyred heroines": Ibid.

88   *Goldberg v. Kelly*, 397 U.S. 54 (1970).

90   "second Emancipation": Martin Luther King, Jr., as quoted in Donald T. Phillips, *Martin Luther King, Jr., on Leadership: Inspiration and Wisdom for Challenging Times* (New York: Warner Books, 1999).

90   "A man should": Martin Luther King, Jr., "Facing the Challenge of a New Age," in Washington, ed., *Testament of Hope*.

95   Marian Wright Edelman, as quoted in Jeff Jacoby, "Welfare reform success," *The Boston Globe*, September 13, 2006.

95   "The Worst Thing": Jeff Jacoby, "Welfare reform success," *The Boston Globe*, September 13, 2006.

FOUR: WHAT WOULD MARTIN SAY ABOUT ILLEGAL IMMIGRATION?

103 "It's ironic": César Chávez, as quoted in Dianne Feinstein, "Statement of Senator Dianne Feinstein: Honoring César Chávez," *Congressional Record: Proceedings and Debates of the 108th Congress, 2nd session*, March 31, 2004 (Washington, D.C.: GPO, 2004).

104 "We seek": César Chávez, as quoted in Otto Santa Ana, *Brown Tide Rising: Metaphors of Latinos in Contemporary American Public* (Austin: University of Texas Press, 2002), 275.

104 "Nonviolence": César Chávez, as quoted in Pepe Lozano, "César Chávez: 'Sî se puede!'" *People's Weekly World*, March 29, 2007.

104 "If you give": César Chávez, "Statement by Cesar Chavez at the End of His Twenty-Four-Day Fast for Justice, Phoenix, Arizona, June 4, 1972," in Richard J. Jensen and John C. Hammerback, eds., *The Words of César Chávez* (College Station: Texas A&M University Press, 2002), 167.

105 "As brothers": Martin Luther King, Jr., as quoted in Richard W. Etulain, ed., *César Chávez: A Brief Biography With Documents* (New York: Palgrave MacMillan, 2002), 81.

106 "During my": César Chávez, *Lessons of Dr. Martin Luther King, Jr.*, The César E. Chávez Foundation, http://www.chavezfoundation.org/speech-g.html (November 17, 2007) [Originally Delivered January 12, 1990].

108 "For so many": César Chávez, as quoted in "Mexican American Voices: César Chávez," *Digital History*, http://www.digitalhistory.uh.edu/mexican_voices/voices_display.cfm?id=110 [Original Source: Hearings Before the Committee on Labor and Human Resources, U.S. Senate, 96th Congress, 1st Session, 1979)].

111 "All persons": *The Constitution of the United States*, Amendment 14.

113 "a civil rights issue": Dennis Byrne, "Immigration issue indeed one of morality," *Chicago Tribune*, August 22, 2006.

113 "I cannot": Elvira Arellano, as quoted in Bill O'Reilly, "America vs. Elvira Arellano," *Fox News.com*, August 21, 2007.

114 "Mexico does not": Felipe Calderón, as quoted in James C. McKinley, Jr., "Mexican President Assails U.S. Measures on Migrants," *The New York Times*, September 3, 2007.

115 "An unjust law": Martin Luther King, Jr., "Letter from Birmingham Jail," in James M. Washington, ed., *A Testament of Hope: The Essential Writings and Speeches of Martin Luther King, Jr.* (San Francisco: Harper Collins, 1991), 294.

115 "I was arrested": Ibid., 294.

119 "sanctuary city": Kareem Fahim, "Presidential Candidate Blames Killings on Newark Sanctuary Policy," *New York Times*, August 21, 2007.

FIVE: WHAT WOULD MARTIN SAY
ABOUT ANTI-SEMITISM?

126 "When I march": Susannah Heschel, "Theological Affinities in the Writings of Heschel and King," in Yvonne Chireau and Nathaniel Deutsch, eds., *Black Zion: African American Religious Encounters with Judaism* (New York: Oxford University Press, 2000), 178–79.

127 "Almost": Martin Luther King, Jr., "Stride Toward Freedom," in James M. Washington, ed., *A Testament of Hope: The Essential Writings of Martin Luther King, Jr.* (San Francisco: Harper Collins, 1991), 482.

127 "the story": Martin Luther King, Jr., "The Birth of a Nation: Sermon Delivered at Dexter Avenue Baptist Church," in Clayborne Carson, Susan Carson, Adrienne Clay, Virginia Shadron, and Kieran Taylor, eds., *Symbol of the Movement*, vol. 4, *The Papers of Martin Luther King, Jr.* (Berkeley: University of California Press, 2005), 155.

127 "been to the mountaintop": Martin Luther King, Jr., "I See the Promised Land," in Washington, ed., *A Testament of Hope*.

128 "I consider": Martin Luther King, Jr., *Keep moving from this mountain*, National Public Radio, http://www.americanrhetoric.com/speeches/mlktempleisraelhollywood.htm (February 26, 1965).

128 "Please demand": Heschel, 178–79.

130 "African movement": Manning Marable, *Black Leadership* (New York: Columbia University Press, 1998), 82.

130 "When people criticize": Martin Luther King, Jr., as quoted in Seymour Martin Lipset, "The Socialism of Fools: The Left, the Jews, & Israel" (New York: Anti-Defamation League, 1969), 7.

131 "Negroes": Martin Luther King, Jr., "Black Power Defined," in Washington, ed., *A Testament of Hope*.

133 James Baldwin, as quoted in "Black Anti-Semitism," *Time*, March 17, 1967.

134 "Black Anti-Semitism," *Time*, March 17, 1967.

134 "were worthy": Louis Farrakhan, as quoted in Robert Singh, *The Farrakhan Phenomenon: Race, Reaction, and the Paranoid Style in American Politics* (Washington, D.C.: Georgetown University Press, 1997), 94.

135 "Well": Martin Luther King, Jr., *Press Conference Following the Assassination of Malcolm X*, Papers of Martin Luther King, Jr., http://www.stanford.edu/group/King/publitions/papers/unpub/650224-000_Malcolm_X_assassination.htm (November 12, 2007). [Original Source: Martin Luther King, Jr. Papers, 1950-1968, Martin Luther King, Jr., Center for Nonviolent Social Change, Inc., (Atlanta), (February 24, 1965)].

135 "reevaluating": Martin Luther King, Jr., "Malcolm X," in Clayborne Carson, ed., *The Autobiography of Martin Luther King, Jr.* (New York: Warner Books, 1998), 268-69.

135 "What you're doing": Malcolm X, as quoted in Nat Hentoff, "Malcolm X vs. Khallid Abdul Muhammad", *Village Voice*, September 30, 1998.

136 "the young men": King, in "Malcolm X,", 268.

136 "Hymietown": Jesse Jackson, as quoted in "Jackson Deplores Threats Against Washington Writer," *New York Times*, April 4, 1984

137 "gutter religion": Louis Farrakhan, as quoted in Hubert G. Locke, *The Black Anti-Semitism Controversy: Protestant Views and Perspectives*, (Cranbury, NJ: Associated University Presses, 1994), 91.

138 "No justice": Al Sharpton, as quoted in Alison Mitchell, "Report Finds An Embattled Crown Heights," *New York Times*, August 19, 1992.

139 "We will not": Al Sharpton, as quoted in "Radio Excerpts in Harlem Store Dispute," *New York Times*, December 14, 1955.

140 "devils": Louis Farrakhan, as quoted in Steven A. Holmes, "Congressional Black Caucus Backs Away from Farrakhan," *New York Times*, February 3, 1994.

140 "synagogue": Louis Farrakhan, as quoted in A. M. Rosenthal, "Kemp and Farrakhan," *New York Times*, October 15, 1996.

140 "the same year": Louis Farrakhan, as quoted in Lisa Singh, "Déjà Vu", *Dallas Observer*, August 10, 2000.

140 Malcolm X, as quoted in Melani McAlister, *Epic Encounters: Culture, Media, and U.S.*

SIX: WHAT WOULD MARTIN SAY ABOUT
ISLAMIC TERRORISM AND THE WAR IN IRAQ?

145 George Wallace, "Statement and Proclamation of Governor George C. Wallace, University of Alabama, June 11, 1963," University of Alabama: June 11, 1963.

145 "Today": John F. Kennedy, "Civil Rights Message," White House: June 11, 1963.

148 "The brutal murder": Martin Luther King, Jr., "A Public Statement," *King Center*, location unspecified, June 12, 1963.

149 "I was to see": David Halberstam, *The Making of a Quagmire* (New York: Random House, 1965).

154 "ethical relativism": Martin Luther King, Jr., *Stride Toward Freedom: The Montgomery Story* (New York: Ballantine Books, 1961).

155 "There is peace": Martin Luther King, Jr., "When Peace Becomes Obnoxious," in Clayborne Carson, Ralph Luker, and Penny A. Russell, eds., *Birth of a New Age*, Vol. 2, The *Papers of Martin Luther King, Jr.* (Berkeley: University of California Press, 1992).

158 "passive": Martin Luther King, Jr., *The Autobiography of Martin Luther King, Jr.* (New York: Warner Books, 1998).

158 "Any man": Malcolm X, as quoted in Peniel E. Joseph, *Waiting 'Til The Midnight Hour: A Narrative History of Black Power in America* (New York: Henry Holt and Co., 2006).

158 "To hell": Stokely Carmichael, as quoted in Martin Luther King, Jr., *Where Do We Go From Here: Chaos or Community?* (New York: Harper & Row, 1967).

158 "power and morality": Martin Luther King, Jr., *Where Do We Go From Here: Chaos or Community?* (New York: Harper & Row, 1967).

159 "Violence": Martin Luther King, Jr., *Keep Moving From This Mountain*, National Public Radio, February 26, 2005.

159 Alfred Nobel, as quoted in Irwin Abrams, "Who Deserves the Nobel Peace Prize?" *Friends Journal* (December 1997).

160 "Whenever": Martin Luther King, Jr., "When Peace Becomes Obnoxious."

161 "I believe": Ibid.

162 "to break": Martin Luther King, Jr., "A Time to Break the Silence," in James M. Washington, ed., *A Testament of Hope: The Essential Writings and Speeches of Martin Luther King, Jr.* (San Francisco: HarperCollins, 1991).

162 "Perhaps": Ibid.

163 "Even": Ibid.

167 "We will turn": Dr. Rachel Ehrenfeld, "The Caliphate Is Coming," *FrontPageMagazine.com*, January 31, 2006.

167 "Bin Laden ordered rocket attacks," *Al Jazeera*, January 13, 2006.

168 "When people": Osama Bin Laden, as quoted in "A Nation Challenged; Scenes of Rejoicing and Words of Strategy From bin Laden and His Allies," *New York Times*, December 14, 2001.

169 "The ruling": Osama Bin Laden, as quoted in Abdullah Saeed, "Trends in Contemporary Islam: A Preliminary Attempt at a Classification," *IkhwanWeb.com*, October 2, 2007.

170 "Zionist-Crusaders": Osama Bin Laden, as quoted in Michael Slackman, "Bin Laden Says West Is Waging War Against Islam," *New York Times*, April 24, 2006.

170 "laugh": Hassan Butt, "My plea to fellow Muslims; you must renounce terror," *The Observer*, July 1, 2007.

172 "worldwide fellowship": Martin Luther King, Jr., "A Time to Break the Silence," in Washington, ed., *A Testament of Hope*.

172 "Beyond": Ibid.

172 "all-embracing": Ibid.

173 "Liberty": Adrian Morgan, "UK: Islamist hate preacher deported," *Spero News*, May 26, 2007.

174 "The way": Ibid.

175 Mick Arran, "The Enemy of My Enemy Is My Friend," *Comments from Left Field*, October 16, 2007.

178 "When our days": Martin Luther King, Jr., *Strength to Love* (New York: Harper & Row, 1963).

SEVEN: WHAT WOULD MARTIN SAY
ABOUT WHO KILLED HIM?

180 "the mistake": Martin Luther King, Jr., "The Albany Movement," in Clayborne Carson, ed., *The Autobiography of Martin Luther King, Jr.* (New York: Warner Books, 1998), 168.

181 "unwise": Martin Luther King, Jr., "Letter from Birmingham Jail," in James M. Washington, ed., *A Testament of Hope: The Essential Writings and Speeches of Martin Luther King, Jr.* (San Francisco: Harper Collins, 1991), 289.

182 "Frankly": Ibid.

183 "our American": J. Edgar Hoover, as quoted in Marty Jezer, *The Dark Ages: Life in the United States 1945-1960* (Boston: South End Press, 1982), 96.

188 Martin Niemoller, as quoted in Ronnie Caplane, "Shoah exhibit reminds FBI of its vow to be vigilant," *Jewish News Weekly of Northern California*, April 3, 1998.

195 "those who": John F. Kennedy, as quoted in Seth Kugel, "Urban Tactics; And Bloomingdale's Returns His Calls," *New York Times*, October 5, 2003.

198 "From December": U.S. Congress, Senate, Select Committee to Study Governmental Operations With Respect to Intelligence Activities, *Supplementary Detailed Staff Reports on Intelligence Activities and the Rights of Americans, Book III, Final Report*, April 23, 1976 (Washington, D.C.: GPO, 1976).

198 W. C. Sullivan, as quoted in John C. Raines, "Righteous Resistance and Martin Luther King, Jr.," *Christian Century*, January 18, 1984.

198 "most dangerous": *Supplementary Detailed Staff Reports.*

199 "extreme": Ibid.

199 "You know": Ibid.

200 "the greatest purveyor": Martin Luther King, Jr., "The Trumpet of Conscience," in Washington, ed., *A Testament of Hope*, 636.

201 "You can bomb": Ibid., 639.

203 "Will B. Outlaw": Allen Salisbury, "Edgar Allan Poe: The Lost Soul of America," *FIDELIO Magazine* Vol. 14 (Spring/Summer 2006).

203 "We no longer": House Committee on Internal Security, 92nd Congress, 2nd Session, U.S. Government Printing Office, Washington, 1972, 9.

204 "Howard B. Franklin": "Faculty Biography: H. Bruce Franklin," *Rutgers University-Newark Department of English* (http://english-newark.rutgers.edu/03_faculty_03_h_bruce_franklin.htm).

204 "something in the air": Desson Thomson, "'The Girl Next Door': Bodies and Brains," *Washington Post*, April 9, 2004.

205 "I'm not a consensus leader": Martin Luther King, Jr., "Remaining Awake Through a Great Revolution," in Washington, ed., *A Testament of Hope*, 276–77.

206 "The anger": Martin Luther King, Jr., from a statement released in Greenwood, Ms, October 14, 1966.

206 Sherrilyn A. Ifill, *On the Courthouse Lawn: Confronting the Legacy of Lynching in the Twenty-First Century* (Boston: Beacon Press, 2007), 58.

209 "Who killed": Martin Luther King, Jr., "A Witness to the Truth," *In Spire* Vol. 6 (Winter 2002), 1–3.

209 "nor is": J. Edgar Hoover, as quoted in Nick Kotz, *Judgment Days: Lyndon Baines Johnson, Martin Luther King, Jr., and the Laws that Changed America* (Boston: Houghton Mifflin Books, 2005), 276.

211 Thomas Carlyle, as quoted by Martin Luther King, Jr., "Remaining Awake Through a Great Revolution," in Washington, ed., *A Testament of Hope*, 277.

211 William Cullen Bryant, as quoted by Martin Luther King, Jr., ibid.

211 James Russell Lowell, as quoted by Martin Luther King, Jr., in Clayborne Carson, Peter Holloran, Ralph Luker, and Penny A. Russell, eds., *Symbol of the Movement*, Vol. 4, *The Papers of Martin Luther King, Jr.* (Berkeley: University of California Press, 2005), 82.